Praise for *The Honeycomb Hypothesis*

The Honeycomb Hypothesis is an essential resource for caregivers of infants and toddlers who strive to offer meaningful interactions between young children and the natural world. The artistry and clarity of this book make the joy, as well as the significance of experiences in nature, come to life.

I loved the helpful hints, Patterns of Play, songs, poems, and activity ideas throughout each section, they are a treasure for educators and parents. Natural and real objects used throughout the book will engage infants and toddlers in learning and provide more sustainable options for teachers. I'm excited to use some of the recipes in our program.

The Honeycomb Hypothesis honors children in all the ways that they express themselves and highlights the important role of a nurturing teacher. The perspectives and deep knowledge offered by the authors bring a solid theoretical foundation together with close observations of young children and teachers to create the honeycomb hypothesis that will help shape the minds, bodies, and hearts of young children. Thank you for your dedication to bringing meaningful experiences with nature to our youngest learners.

—**Sheila Williams Ridge**, Child Development Laboratory School, University of Minnesota

The Honeycomb framework invites us into the fascinating world of young children's natural play and learning through a combination of research and simple, practical suggestions. Based on Jean Piaget's theory of cognitive development and Edward O. Wilson's theory of biophilia we are led into a wonderous natural world all children have the right to explore and be immersed in. This treasure is filled with helpful notes, simple recipes and jewels of information and knowledge. A book that should be required reading for anyone working with young children.

—**Niki Buchan**, International Educational Consultant, Natural Learning Early Childhood Consultancy

The Honeycomb Hypothesis is the perfect title for a book rich in creativity. The book overflows with exciting ideas and interesting analogies about how infants, toddlers and twos learn and grow. While a hypothesis in some situations may keep you guessing, this book doesn't. From the philosophical framework presented in Part I, to the more than one hundred nature-based activities offered in Part II, to the "pulling it all together" discussion in Part III, this book is sure to give readers a clear roadmap for enriching the lives of very young children.

—**Ruth Wilson, Ph.D.**, Research Library Curator, Children and Nature Network, Author of *Nature and Young Children* and *Learning Is In Bloom*

This is a must-have for any educator aiming to support nature-based learning among our youngest children! As the nature-based education movement grows there are more and more educators wondering how to connect the youngest children to nature. Is it even possible? This book makes it clear the answer is absolutely Yes! The authors have beautifully described the many ways infants, toddlers, and two-year-olds engage with the natural world. They also provide clear, concrete ideas for materials and interactions for developmentally appropriate and child-centered ways to extend play. This is exactly the book our field was needing.

—**Rachel A. Larimore, Ph.D.**, Author of *Preschool Beyond Walls: Blending Nature-Based Learning and Early Childhood Education*

The Honeycomb Hypothesis takes us on a wondrous journey of learning, exploration and creativity by connecting nature to playful learning. Using the analogy of the honeybee, we see the world through the eyes of the child—buzzing from stimuli, to experiences, to discovery, to skill and knowledge development. This book is overflowing with information and insight that prompt us to reflect on our practice as educators. The authors have relied on extensive research and experience to guide us through practical and common sense solutions for all early childhood classrooms as we get to know more about patterns of play and why they are important.

—**Kathryn Murray, Ph.D.**, Future Strong Education Consultancy, Australia

Sandra Duncan, EdD, Sue Penix and Sally Haughey

THE HONEYCOMB HYPOTHESIS

How Infants, Toddlers and Two-Year-Olds Learn Through Nature Play

Exchange Press

ISBN 978-0-942702-79-8

© 2022 Sandra Duncan, Sue Penix and Sally Haughey

Book Design: Kaitlyn Nelsen
Production Design: Stacy Hawthorne
Editor: Erin Glenn

This book may not be reproduced in whole or in part by any means without written permission of the publisher.

For more information about other Exchange Press publications and resources for directors and teachers, contact:

Exchange Press
7700 A Street
Lincoln, NE 68510
(800) 221-2864
ExchangePress.com

Dimensions Educational Research Foundation and Exchange Press cannot be held responsible for damage, mishap, or injury incurred during the use of or because of the activities in this book. Appropriate and reasonable caution and adult supervision of children involved in activities and corresponding to the age and capability of each child involved are recommended at all times. Do not leave children unattended at any time. When making choices about allowing children to touch or eat certain foods, plants, or flowers, make sure to investigate possible toxicity and consider any food allergies or sensitivities. Observe safety and caution at all times.

DEDICATION

This book is dedicated to our grandchildren who are our honey bees and light of our lives.
They inspire us to be our best and fly high each and every day.

Adalena & Julie
Sue's grandchildren

Sierra Elizabeth
Sandra's grandchild

Kaiden & Kamden
Sally's grandchildren

A million moments strung together like dewdrops on a spiderweb, every moment contributes to the whole child's experience of the world. If we could put our finger on the essence of childhood, we would discover its magic embodied in the natural world. The sweetness of a honeysuckle blossom. Hungry yips of fox cubs. Water chasing and racing down a creekbed. The banter of blue jays. Carefree butterflies dancing on the wind. The daring tree stunts of squirrels. The arresting stillness of a blinky, starry night. The warm embrace of sunshine.

FOREWORD

Play and exploration in nature are both central to a child's development and also a mirror for how they grow in, and of, the natural world.

The positive effects of time spent in nature are undeniable. A range of developmental skills are enhanced. But deeper still are the social, emotional, and spiritual domains that we tap into, when children discover their oneness with the natural world. This bond is essential, literally at the essence of our being, and awakened through play and time spent outdoors. Decisions regarding our health, nutrition, schools, families, native lands, cultures and, indeed, our world, hinge upon this essential bond. Children become stronger, healthier, happier, and more empathetic when they engage in frequent outdoor learning. The same is true for adults.

As parents, teachers, and caregivers, we have the sacred responsibility of helping children blossom into being. This book offers many ways to savor moments and experience wonder together through hands-on learning opportunities, all born from nature. Here you will discover ideas to help children engage in nature-based learning, all while supporting essential skill development. Gear up for wonderful adventures and don't be surprised if you stir up your own curiosity along the way!

Monica Wiedel-Lubinski
Executive Director
Eastern Region Association of Forest and Nature Schools

CONTENTS

PART I — THE HONEYCOMB FRAMEWORK

THE HONEYCOMB FRAMEWORK:
OUR JOURNEY 15

THE HONEYCOMB HYPOTHESIS 19
    Patterns of Nature 19
    Patterns of Play 19
    The Honey Bee's Journey 22
    Players in The Honeycomb
       Hypothesis 26
    Pedagogical Practices for The
       Honeycomb Hypothesis 29
    Strategies for Supporting Children's
       Patterns of Play 33

BORN TO EXPERIENCE THE WORLD 37
    Young Children are
       Meaning Makers 37
    Natural Materials are
       Meaning Makers 38
    Tips for Collecting Nature 41
    Safety and Precautions for Nature
       Explorations 41

PART II — EXPLORING THROUGH ACTIVITIES

EXPLORING THROUGH ACTIVITIES:
CHILD-LED LEARNING WITH
NATURE'S BOUNTY 47

EXCEPTIONAL EARTH 48
    Connecting with Earth 51
    Elemental Earthing 51
Dynamic Dirt 52
    Dirt Detectives 53
    Dirt Piles 53
    Dirt Tracks 55
Marvelous Mud 56
    Mud Paint 58
    Mud Sensory Table 59
    Mud Masterpieces 60
    Mud Walk 61
    Mud Dough 62
    Mud Cooking 63
    Mud Kitchens 65
Creative Clay 68
    Clay Table 71
    Clay Tray 71
    Clay Bin 71
    Clay Board 72
    Clay Tree Stump 73
    Clay Boulder 73
    Clay-pressions 74
    Clay Painting 74
    Clay Sculptures 77
    Clay Blankets 78
Simply Sand 80
    Fill and Spill 82
    Sand Sacks 83
    Sand Trays 84

Significant Stones 87
    Reach for a Rock 88
    Stone Marking 90
    Stone Hideaways 92
    Let's Play 93
    Stone Stacking 94
    Roll a Rock 95
Mark Making 97
    Mark Making on the Go 98
    Spray Chalking 99
    Chalk Marking 100
    Paint Brush Marking 102
Magic Metal 104
    Metal Clay Sculptures 105
    Potato Masher Prints 105
    Bucket Brigade 105
    Nesting Metal Bowls 106
    Metal Mirrors 107
Perfect Pathways 109
    Tree Cookie Pathways 109
    Circular Stone Pathways 110
    Short-Grass Pathways 112
    Textured Pathways 114

WONDROUS WATER 116
Rain Puddles and Water Fun 119
    Water Painting 120
    Washing Day 122
    Fill 'Em Up 124
    Icicle Painting 126
    Flower Ice Sculptures 128
Squishy Sea Sponges 130
    Sponge Squeeze 131
    Sponge Walk 132
    Sponge Splatter 133
Beautiful Bubbles 134
    Beautiful Bubble Recipe 137
    Whisking Bubbles 138
    Bubble Painting 139

Special Seashells 141
    Seashell Sounds 141
    Stringing Seashells 142
    All in a Row 142
    Clamshell Painting 143
    Seashell Small World 143

FANTASTIC FLORA & FAUNA 144
Lofty Leaves 147
    Catch a Leaf 147
    Classroom Fun with Leaves 148
    Leaf Angels 150
    Leaf Transporting 151
    Leaf Marking 153
    Leaf Prints 153
    Autumn Hunt 154
    Sunny Leaf Catchers 155
    Crunchy Crunch 156
Tremendous Trees 159
    Gifts to Trees 159
    Tree Bark Marking 160
    Tree Peek-a-Boo 161
    Tree Cookies 162
Bountiful Birds 166
    Inviting Birds to Visit 167
    Bird Feeders 168
    Hummingbird Heaven 170
    Hummingbird Food 171
    Bird Nest Discovery Bin 172
    Nesting Gifts 173
Glorious Grass 174
    Grass Stew 176
    Grass Bracelet 177
    Bamboo Marking 177
Growing Gardens 179
    Mini-Gardens 180
    Portable Gardens 180
    Sensory Gardens 182
    Wall Gardens 184

Pallet Herb Gardens	185
Kitchen Scrap Gardens	186
Stupendous Sticks	189
Stick Weavings	190
Collage on a Stick	191
Painted Sticks	191
Sticky Stick Sculptures	192
Pretty Pinecones	194
Pinecone Palooza	195
Pretty Pinecone Presents	196
Shake and Make Pine Cones	197
Kerplink-Kerplunk	198
Turkey Baster Pine Cones	199
Delightful Dandelions	200
Dandelion Soup	201
Dandelion Dough	201
Dandelion Weaving	202
Dandelion Bouquets	202
Line 'Em Up	203
Playful Pumpkins	204
Pumpkin Boats	204
Pumpkin Painting	204
Carrying and Stacking Pumpkins	205
Sunny Sunflowers	207
Light Table Sunflower	207
Sunflower Prints	208
Pulling Petals	209
Wiggly Worms	210
Worm Watching	210
Worm Digging	211
Worm Terrarium	211
Flutterby Butterflies	212
Caterpillar Crawl	214
Butterfly Dance	215
Butterfly Feeders	215
CONNECTING WITH CONCOCTIONS	216
Getting Started with Concocting	219
Mortar and Pestle: Concocting Tool	222
Chalk Concoctions	224
Chalk Ice	225
Chalk Clay	225
Chalk Sand	226
Wet Chalk	227
Paint Concoctions	228
Berry Paint	229
Sand Concoctions	231
Texture Concoctions	232
Fairy Stew	233
Petal Potions	233
Meadow Paint	234
Potpourri Dough	234
Herbed Clay Dough	235

PART III — PUTTING IT ALL TOGETHER

PUTTING IT ALL TOGETHER: ENVIRONMENT, MATERIALS, AND PEDAGOGY	239
The Honey Bee's Learning Environment	239
The Honeycomb Hypothesis and Piaget: Exploring to Learn	244
The Honey Bee's Flight Pattern to Understanding	245
Novelty is the Pedagogy of the Third Teacher	245
AN INVITATION: TAKE FLIGHT WITH HONEY BEES	248
ACKNOWLEDGEMENTS	250
ABOUT THE AUTHORS	253
RESOURCES	254
CREDITS	258

PART 1

THE HONEYCOMB
FRAMEWORK

THE HONEYCOMB FRAMEWORK: OUR JOURNEY

As a team of three authors we have wide-ranging experience in learning and growing with children and families around the world. We are committed to our own lifelong learning and seeking new understandings as we teach and live. Writing this book has been an incredible journey for us as we studied, observed and explored alongside young children and their teachers—always deepening our grasp of infants, toddlers, and two-year-olds, and how these marvelous beings gain understanding and construct meanings of the world around them.

Although this learning journey led us down many pathways, we apply two theoretical and conceptual frameworks to the book: Jean Piaget's theory of cognitive development and Edward O. Wilson's theory of biophilia.

Jean Piaget's (1896-1980) theory of cognitive development offers tremendous insight on how children construct knowledge and gain understanding. Piaget studied and illuminated the process through which children explore and integrate new experiences, to make sense of the world and form their own unique understandings.

Edward O. Wilson's theory of biophilia celebrates human beings' innate attraction to life itself, as expressed through the natural world and all living things. Human beings have a basic and essential affinity to nature and natural elements, and are inspired and healed through interrelationship with nature.

As educators, and as human beings, we view the power of nature as the ultimate facilitator in supporting children's learning. We want to support and encourage teachers to engage and align with nature every day, and offer abundant opportunities to children, in service of our shared growth, inspiration, health, and joy.

We discuss children's learning through the vocabulary of schemes and schemas. While there are many definitions of "schema" in the academic world, we signify scheme and schema as the following:

OUR DEFINITIONS OF SCHEME AND SCHEMA		
SCHEME (Patterns of Play)	• External actions • Visible • Observable	Schemes are Patterns of Play that are observable and repetitive movements or actions children engage in during play. Patterns of Play are children's innate and insatiable urges to explore and experience the world around them. This book focuses on six Patterns of Play: *Making & Unmaking*, *Hiding & Revealing*, *Carrying & Placing*, *Attaching & Detaching*, *Turning & Stopping*, *Propelling & Hindering*.
SCHEMA (Mental Models)	• Internal process • Not Visible	Schemas are internal frameworks for understanding. Schemas are present in the mind of every individual. They are the mental organization of the bits and pieces of data that children gather when engaging in the Patterns of Play.

THE HONEYCOMB FRAMEWORK

As early childhood educators, we cannot see the actual process of learning—it is invisible. We cannot see children's schemas or observe their internal processing of information. We cannot know why or where children will store their uniquely personal bits and pieces of collected information. We can support children's growth and exploration by observing and encouraging the Patterns of Play. We can offer experiences, materials and opportunities to provoke and invite children—which enhances their invisible, inward formation of new understandings. This journey of observation, provocation and following the children's lead inspires and honors children's innate intelligence, and the process is delightful.

We invite you to join us in the world of patterns of play, schemas, honey bees, infants, toddlers, and two-year-old children. Use the rich hands-on experiences and ideas for fostering young children's growth and joy through open-ended nature exploration. Experience the joy of watching the young honey bees in your classroom fly to new and inspiring heights.

Sandra Duncan, EdD, Sue Penix and Sally Haughey

Theory Versus Hypothesis

There is a distinct difference between the words "theory" and "hypothesis." A theory is a tested, verified, and substantiated explanation of a phenomenon.

What we are presenting has not been tested or researched in a formal setting. The purpose of this book is to present a possibility of how children learn, to be further explored and investigated.

THE HONEYCOMB HYPOTHESIS

Patterns of Nature

With unfailing consistency and regularity, the seasons come and go, the sun rises and falls, and the tide comes in and goes out. Predictable patterns in nature are expressed not only through these rhythms, but also through majestic patterns such as spirals in conch seashells, stripes of zebras, facets of snowflakes, and beautiful designs on the wings of monarchs.

Children experience similar growth patterns. Some growth patterns are overwhelmingly obvious such as baby's first steps. On the other hand, some patterns of growth are subtle and almost impossible to understand in a singular moment in time such as a toddler dumping all the contents of every basket from the nearby shelf onto the floor. It is only when we are able to stand back and observe the way children play that we begin to understand the intensity and purpose of their actions.

Children's evolution of learning is not just a single moment in time but a collection of moments, hours, days, months, and years. A sunflower opens and closes its petals every day. Observing this daily phenomenon might cause you to overlook the sunflower's ever-growing height. And, if you blink you may miss the sunflower's other marvelous wonders because of its rapid growth. Yet, the sunflower predictably repeats its daily rituals, opening and shutting, and continues to reach for the sun. The same is true for young children: They are marvelous beings that grow and learn from repetitive behaviors over a collection of many moments in time. These repetitive behaviors are called Patterns of Play.

Patterns of Play

Play is the essence of early childhood. Young children are born compelled by a natural instinct to play. It is through play that babies, toddlers, and two-year-old children learn about the world around them. There is something very interesting about how young children play. Observe closely and you will notice children exhibiting repetitive movements or actions. For example, you may see an industrious toddler filling up a bucket—only to immediately dump its contents out and continue to repeat the process over and over again. You may observe a child stacking up blocks and repeatedly knocking them down with a gleeful smile on her face. Or you may experience a small child dropping his sippy cup over the edge of the high chair and, after you retrieve it for the umpteenth time, dropping it again. Although these repetitive behaviors, or Patterns of Play, may seem inconsequential and oftentimes frustrating, children are actually building the capacities of their brains and constructing knowledge or understandings when they engage in these innate actions and behaviors.

So, what do these Patterns of Play look like? How do they exhibit themselves in young children? This book focuses on six repetitive movements or actions that teachers of infants, toddlers, and two-year-old children most likely observe on a daily basis. Recognizing and understanding these Patterns of Play helps you to better understand children's behaviors. More importantly, recognizing these repetitive behaviors helps to create developmentally appropriate experiences designed to encourage Patterns of Play and thereby promote children's understandings.

Children build understanding through their own actions and interactions with the immediate world including both built environments (i.e., classrooms and homes) and the outdoor space (i.e., forest or woods, parks, backyards, and beyond). Patterns of Play are the actions children use to build understandings or concepts in these environments. A thorough grasp of how the world works requires children to have many opportunities and a variety of experiences so they can begin: (1) collecting a multitude of bits and pieces of information; (2) storing this collected information in their brains; and, (3) making connections between the bits and pieces of information they have collected with the data stored in their brains in order to construct schemas or mental models. A wise teacher provides many different types of play opportunities with a variety of interesting materials and in different environments or spaces, helping young children to:

- Strengthen already built knowledge.
- Explore and interact with fascinating materials/objects to develop new knowledge or concepts.
- Expand the connection between previously learned concepts and new knowledge.

One way to successfully accomplish these three types of play opportunities is by providing nature-based experiences. This book invites you to begin supporting infants, toddlers, and two-year-old children's innate urges or Patterns of Play by offering extraordinary nature-based experiences designed to spark imagination, curiosity, and discovery. It is important to note that "action schemas" were first identified in *Extending Thought in Young Children: A Parent-Teacher Partnership* by Chris Athey.[1] Although there are many more, this book focuses on six Patterns of Play, which are: *(1) Making & Unmaking; (2) Hiding & Revealing; (3) Carrying & Placing; (4) Attaching & Detaching; (5) Turning & Stopping; and, (6) Propelling & Hindering.*

1. Athey, C. *Extending Thought in Young Children: A Parent-Teacher Partnership.* Los Angeles, CA: Sage Publications, 2007.

PATTERNS OF PLAY

MAKING & UNMAKING	The **making urge** is one of mixing, stirring, swirling, crushing, constructing, inventing, designing, and building. The child is repeating an action of **making** something.	The **unmaking urge** is knocking down, spreading, smashing, pinching, poking and banging. These are the repeated actions of **unmaking** something.
HIDING & REVEALING	The **hiding urge** is about filling, burying, covering, wrapping, or concealing. The child is repeating an action of **hiding** or containing something; it's a function of not seeing.	The **revealing urge** is uncovering, dumping, showing, unwrapping, unearthing, unveiling, and presenting. It is a repeated action of **revealing** something; it's a function of seeing.
CARRYING & PLACING	The **carrying urge** is gathering, digging, picking up, carrying, pouring, and holding. It's a repeated action of picking things up, moving, and **carrying**. It's also the essential urge to change one's body perspective through movement.	The **placing urge** is scattering, handing, putting, setting, positioning and lying down. The child is repeating the actions of **placing** something somewhere. It is also the primary urge of placing one's body in a certain space or position.
ATTACHING & DETACHING	The **attaching urge** is piling, stacking, joining together, lining things up, gluing, pasting, tying, linking, sticking, and arranging. There is a repeated urge to **attach** and put things together.	The **detaching urge** is pulling, tearing, or cutting apart, undoing, and peeling away. The child is repeating an action of **detaching** things from each other.
TURNING & STOPPING	The **turning urge** is spinning, turning around, twirling, or running in circles. It is also exhibited with small body movements such as the turning of knobs or screws, twisting on lids, or rolling toys with wheels. There is a repeated urge to move, rotate, and **turn** in a circular motion.	The **stopping urge** is freezing, ending, discontinuing motion, standing still, and halting. **Stopping** is the primary urge to stop the circular motion of an object or oneself.
PROPELLING & HINDERING	The **propelling urge** is throwing, tossing, rolling, racing, pushing, jumping, darting, dashing, flying, and whizzing. There is a repeated urge of **propelling** an object or oneself in space.	The **hindering urge** is waiting, hesitating, postponing, lagging behind, delaying, creeping, tiptoeing, and dragging. **Hindering** is the primary urge of delaying or slowing down movement of an object or oneself in space.

The Honey Bee's Journey

Have you ever observed honey bees flitting around and nosing up to sweet smelling flowers? Pause to observe them and you may notice just how these little wonders of nature are busily gathering pollen to carry back to their hives. This repeated gathering, collecting, taking, and placing the pollen in the hive is innate and instinctive. Honey bees happily buzz back and forth, back and forth, and repeat the process so quickly you may grow dizzy as you observe.

Keep your eyes on the honey bee's journey. After the bee has gathered as much pollen as it can possibly carry, it returns to the hive and performs an observable happy dance of communication. Known as

the waggle dance, these motions communicate to fellow bees knowledge learned about where to find the most delicious flowers. The little dancer delivers the pollen to the worker bees in the honeycomb. In addition to food for the Queen, the worker bees may decide to put the collected pollen in an already existing food storage cell or it may be used to create a new cell in the honeycomb.

Much like bees, young children also search and forage their environments for bits and pieces of information. This search is conducted through Patterns of Play. For example, a child who repeatedly carries a pumpkin back and forth across the playground and places it on a tree stump is exhibiting the *Carrying & Placing* Pattern of Play. Through these repetitive actions, the child is storing information and building knowledge about the pumpkin's properties and practicing concepts such as weight and balance. Similar to the honey bee deciding how to use the foraged pollen, a child's brain processes and stores information gleaned from both built and outdoor environments. The child determines how this knowledge (or concept) fits into his understandings and where it will be stored for future use.

24 THE HONEYCOMB FRAMEWORK

Picture a honeycomb as a child's brain with each cell of the honeycomb containing concepts or mental models learned through Patterns of Play. Mud play, for example, gives a young child many opportunities and ways to practice the *Making & Unmaking* Pattern of Play. As the child messes about and plays with the mud, she experiences its unique properties or concepts such as its gooeyness, stickiness, and squishiness. Through this play experience, the child is constructing understandings and much like the honey bee, making unconscious decisions about where to store her personal and individualized gathered data about the mud:

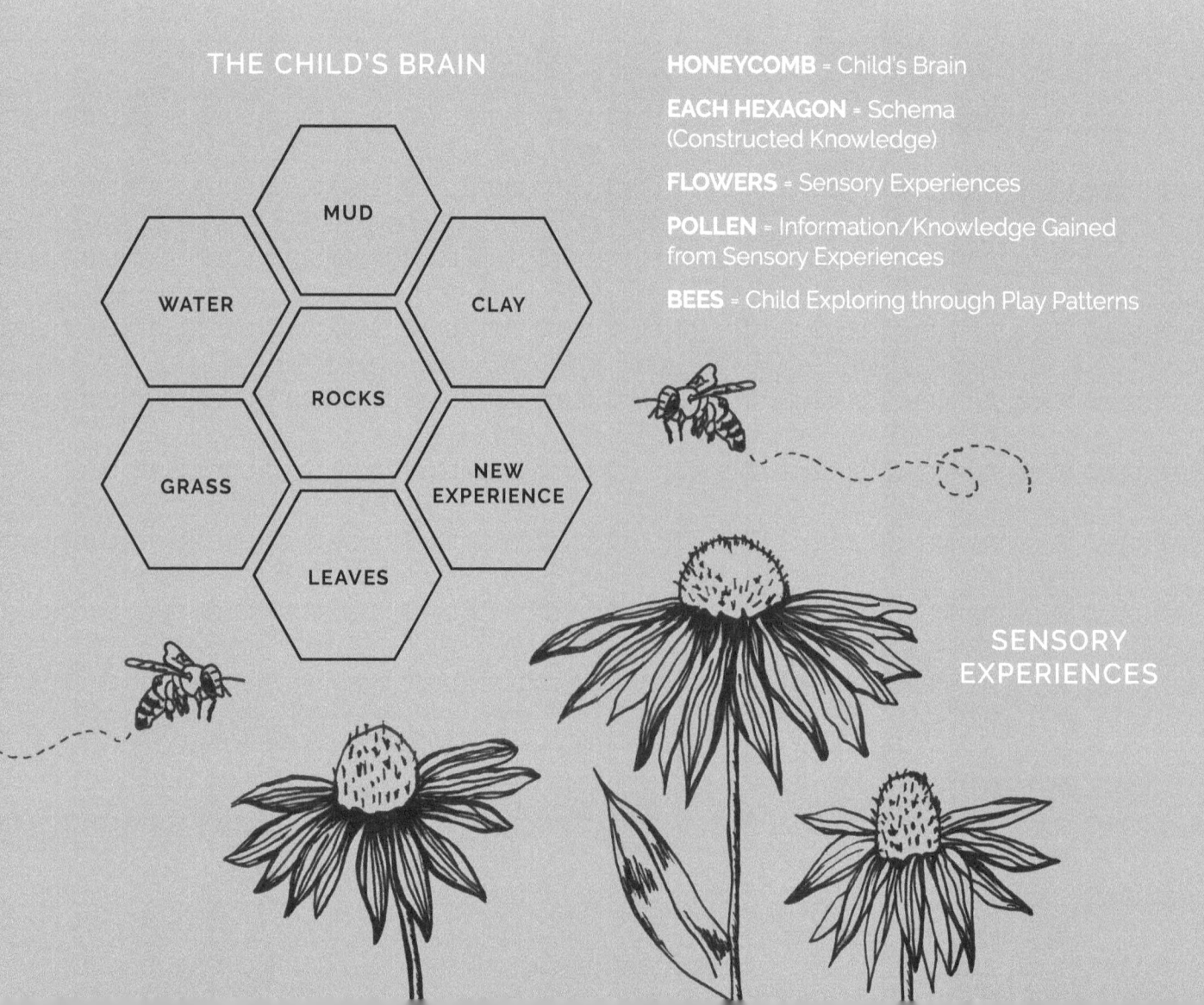

1. Because the young thinker had chocolate pudding for lunch that day, she may decide to assimilate the concept of mud into her pre-existing schema of chocolate pudding and put the mud into the pudding section of the brain's honeycomb.

2. The child might accommodate the notion of mud by altering her pre-existing schema of chocolate pudding and put the mud into the chocolate pudding schema.

3. The child may determine that the mud doesn't fit in the pudding schema (or anywhere!) and thus create a new cell in the honeycomb in order to accomodate the concept of mud.

Indeed, there are many ways a child can create and store his personal understandings about mud. The problem is this: Unless we are researchers and have access to brain imaging, we cannot see into a child's thought process. We cannot begin to know why or where a child will store his uniquely personal bits and pieces of mud data. And, let's consider this thought to muddy the waters: Having painted with brown finger paint two days prior to experiencing the mud, the child may decide to store the mud paint into a whole new honeycomb of *painting*. We just don't know.

So, now that you understand a little bit about The Honeycomb Hypothesis, what does this mean? The answer is simple:

> The honey bees in your classroom need pollen from many different varieties of flowers—or many different hands-on experiences with nature—so they have enough to feed themselves and build their brain's honeycomb.

> The greater the variety of materials offered (especially natural materials) such as pinecones, sticks, stones, mud, sand, seashells, and clay . . . the more opportunities children have to explore, transform, and engage in the different Patterns of Play. As they combine materials together and take them apart again and again, they are engaging in Patterns of Play and learning all they can about the many properties of the materials. In turn, children are placing, filling up, and building honeycombs as they assimilate and accommodate newfound information into their brains.

Players in The Honeycomb Hypothesis

The Forager Honey Bee 	The honey bee is representative of young children who fly about exploring every nook and cranny of their built and outdoor environments. Exploring their worlds through observable Patterns of Play (i.e., *Attaching & Detaching; Hiding & Revealing*) helps young children build understandings that can be brought back to their honeycombs (brains) to store for future use and learning.
Flight of the Honey Bee 	The flight of honey bees foraging for pollen is instinctive and focused. These actions are much like young children's purposeful and repetitive movements when they are engaged in Patterns of Play. As children actively explore their worlds and engage in repetitive movements, they are gathering bits and pieces of information about the materials with which they are playing. Children take all this data and create understandings or schemas about a concept such as the properties of mud (i.e., color, feel, smell).
 The Honeycomb and Worker Bees	The individual chambers in the honey bee's comb represent the mental models (or schemas) in the child's brain. The honeycomb's hexagonal cells are all connected—just like the bits and pieces of new information are incorporated and connected to form a child's unique understandings. Each cell of the honeycomb is representative of a schema (or concept) and is the foundation for the child's understandings. Each hexagonal cell of the honeycomb is connected and related to all the other cells. In the honeycomb, it is the job of a worker bee to be the gatekeeper of the honeycomb and (1) to accept the collected pollen; (2) make unconscious decisions about where to place the foraged materials (i.e., add to an existing cell, build a new cell); and, (3) to begin making connections between chambers. With the child, the process of assimilating and accommodating environmental data is representative of the activity that stimulates the neuron firing to make synaptic connections in the brain.

The Waggle Dance 	The honey bee's waggle dance happens when it returns to the hive. During this dance, the forager bee offers "smells" so other bees learn of the pollen's quality. The dancing honey bee also communicates the direction and distance of the foraged material. The waggle dance is akin to a child's excitement in self-discovery.
The Hive 	The hive is the home of the bees. It is the place in which eggs are laid, hatched, nurtured and raised. It is the honey bees' safe place from storms, heat, wind, and cold. The hive is a complex structure composed of many small connecting combs and is representative of a child's world, which also has many connections, relationships, and interrelationships with the environment and others such as family, community, and school.
The Honey Gardener 	The honey gardener is the child's teacher. In the analogy of The Honeycomb Hypothesis, the honey gardener cares for, cultivates, and tends to the flower garden by watering, weeding, and planting new flowers for the bees to enjoy. Just as the honey gardener cares for and tends to the garden and hive, so does the teacher prepare and tend the classroom environment by cultivating a special place where young children's interests and developmental needs are met through play. It is the honey gardener who observes the children at play, notes their interests, makes adjustments to the environment, and offers a variety of new experiences intentionally designed to extend children's understandings or schemas.

Pedagogical Practices for The Honeycomb Hypothesis

Have you heard the saying "busy as a bee"? Observe a honey bee and it seems to be in constant motion: flying here, flying there—back and forth from the flower to the hive—back and forth, back and forth. When flowers are in bloom, it seems that the bee's job of carrying pollen from one flower to another is never done. The same is true for young children. Like honey bees, they fly about the classroom and outdoor environments foraging for information. The Honeycomb Hypothesis encourages three strategies for motivating children's flight patterns: (1) Heuristic Play; (2) The Three I's; and, (3) Flying Outside the Lines.

(1) HEURISTIC PLAY

In the 1980's English educationalist Elinor Goldschmeid (1910-2009) conceived the term "Heuristic Play" to describe young children as they play with real world objects through their senses. Goldschmeid believed in the importance of offering natural materials to children. These natural materials and objects invite endless possibilities for children's exploring, learning, and discovering. Goldschmeid felt the way in which the objects were presented to young children was of utmost importance. She advocated for presenting the materials in baskets or natural containers and placing them on the floor, high chair tray, or table top as an invitation for play. Through manipulating, exploring, and experimenting, it was Goldschmeid's idea that young children acquire knowledge or develop schemas through the characteristics (i.e. texture, shapes, smells and colors) of the natural materials. With Heuristic Play, children are the leaders of their own play with natural materials, which is sparked by their own imaginations and innate desire to explore.

Heuristic experiences provide even the smallest child with opportunities to practice Patterns of Play. Repeated actions such as gathering, pouring, and dumping while engaged in Heuristic Play fulfill the primary urge to transform materials by doing and undoing. If you look closely and observe quietly, you may be lucky enough to get a glimpse into the honey bee's (child's) flight pattern and begin to understand the invisible workings of the honeycomb (child's brain) that are being harnessed by Heuristic Play.

(2) THE THREE "I'S"

Think of the Patterns of Play as the framework for children's learning. The building blocks for this framework are (1) Imagination; (2) Innovation; and, (3) Invention. As children learn about their world through the properties of natural materials, they fill out their frameworks.

1. **Imagination.** Children use their imaginations while engaging in Patterns of Play. When thinking about children's imaginations, our minds typically gravitate to make-believe play. Pretend play is considered to be a staple of early childhood and primarily thought of as an avenue for social and emotional development. But, contrary to this belief, imaginative play is also a cognitive process. The child who is pretending to be a farmer, for example, is constructing Piaget's mental models (i.e., garden, barn, animals) of the farming world. These mental models are progressive and ever-changing as the play evolves. Constantly taking information gained from the imaginative farm scenes, the child applies, organizes, and reorganizes the data in order to create understandings about the farm.

2. **Innovation.** Children innovate when engaged in the repetitive movements that make up the Patterns of Play. Children's play is all about experimenting—trying out new ways to engage and manipulate the environment and the objects within it. This is known as innovation in play. For example, a child playing with round stones might exhibit all sorts of innovative play: stacking the stones in a tall pile, lining up a pile of same-sized rocks in a straight row, or selecting all the gray rocks from a pile and rolling them down a ramp. Through these play innovations, young children are discovering how the stones look, feel, and react in each of these different situations. Innovations with play are not about learning a prescribed body of knowledge (i.e., knowledge about gravity and momentum, or size and color discrimination). They are not about an inventory of stored information. Rather, innovation is a process; it is a repertoire of actions, which cause changes in children's mental models that mirror or reflect their play experiences.[2]

3. **Invention.** Children's innovations lead to inventions. Invention is figuring out a way to do something original or creating a unique product, method, or process. For example, because Jimmy wants to catch a fish at his grandma's lake, he may invent a fishing pole by taping some string to a stick and using a paperclip for the hook. Jimmy's invention of the fishing pole was first grounded in imagination. His imagination proceeded on to innovation, and finally to inventing as he adjusted his mental model of an authentic fishing pole.

2. Piaget, J. *Psychology and Epistemology: Towards a Theory of Knowledge.* London: Routledge & Kegan Paul, *1972.*

PATTERNS OF PLAY: THE THREE "I'S"

IMAGINATION

INVENTION   INNOVATION

PLAY

Piaget believed that "all knowledge is continually in a course of development and of passing from a state of lesser knowledge to one which is more complete and effective." This is why young children are in a constant state of invention. They like to make stuff, mix and combine materials, put together, and take apart. All of these actions (or Patterns of Play) are children's innate responses to transition from Piaget's state of lesser knowledge to a state of improved knowledge. In reality, young children are organizing and reorganizing their mental models just as Jimmy did when he invented the fishing pole.

(3) FLYING OUTSIDE THE LINES

When we were young, the majority of us were instructed and taught how to color within the lines. We worked hard with our tiny fingers tightly squeezing the jumbo crayon, our tongues in our cheeks, trying to stay within the lines on the coloring page. Although we really didn't understand why it was so important to stay within the lines, most of us were determined to accomplish the task in a good enough way to earn a gold star or a happy face from our teacher. Just like yesteryear, rote learning, memorization, and repetitious thinking are confining many of today's young honey bees. They are not allowed or given opportunities to fly outside the lines. As early childhood educators, it is up to us to change and to create a new mindset: *Knowing is Not Understanding*.

Knowing is Not Understanding. Just because a child has memorized and can sing the alphabet song without missing a beat doesn't mean he understands the nuances of the alphabet. Just because a child can count to 50 doesn't mean she understands numeracy—it just means she has a good memory. Rather than promoting confinement of children's brains by staying within the lines of rote memorization, let's help young honey bees fly outside the lines and create their own meaningful learning.

KNOWING IS NOT UNDERSTANDING

Staying Within the Lines =
Rote Learning

Flying Outside the Lines =
Meaningful Learning

There is a lot of talk out there about "meaningful learning," but exactly what does it mean? Although children are meaning makers, meaning is not a given state of affairs, nor is it static. Rather, it is an intimate and continual transaction that occurs between a child and the environment. It is the relationship between environmental information and its recipient. Ultimately, a child's meaning is personal and only exists within the individual. Consequently, it is impossible to observe meaning.

When children make meaning, we cannot witness Piaget's accommodation and assimilation and the changes that occur within a child's mental models. Meaning can be revealed, in part, through observing children's Patterns of Play. Even then, we as adults can only suppose how children make meaning and can only guess if we are providing meaningful learning experiences for them. It would seem that the best possible action for early childhood educators to take is to step down and let the child take the lead. Like the waggle dance of the honey bee that tells the other bees where to find the best pollen, let the child show us where she is determined to fly.

Strategies for Supporting Children's Patterns of Play

Knowing why children exhibit repetitive behaviors and understanding the significance of these actions is beneficial for all teachers. Rather than becoming frustrated with a toddler continually swiping the toys off shelves or a two-year-old spilling the container's contents onto the floor (after you have just picked up the room), you now know children are exhibiting these repetitive behaviors because they are innate urges and direct routes to creating understandings. Knocking down a small tower of soft blocks over and over again helps children gather and store bits and pieces of information that transform into schemas, or understandings.

Now that you are aware of Patterns of Play and understand their importance in young children's acquisition of knowledge, you may be thinking: How can I support these naturally occurring play urges? In supporting children's Patterns of Play, there are several important teacher practices to remember:

- Give children uninterrupted time and space to explore.
- Expand children's vocabulary by using descriptive words.
- Provide tools for joyous play.

Successful teachers understand that children's interests motivate learning so they pay attention to the ideas children express in their play and adjust their pedagogical practices accordingly. The Honeycomb Hypothesis recommends three methods for responding and supporting children's Patterns of Play: (1) Pure Exploration; (2) Narrated Exploration; and, (3) Transformational Exploration.

(1) PURE EXPLORATION

Pure exploration is pure joy . . . and happens when a child is completely immersed with materials in the environment. Pure exploration is re-imagining, re-situating, and "re-alizing" the possibilities of the world. The key to promoting children's pure exploration is simple:

> **BEST PRACTICE FOR PURE EXPLORATION:** Let children's natural instincts take over.

- Keep it child-led, which means the child (and not the teacher) leads the way to play.

- Provide generous inside and outside space for exploration experiences.

- Offer captivating and novel materials, which isn't hard to do with very young children since most everything in their world is new.

- Give the gift of uninterrupted time and personal thought, which means there are large chunks of time with little (if any) verbal interjections from you when children are engaged in pure exploration.

(2) NARRATED EXPLORATION

Narrated exploration is using intentional language that helps young children connect ideas, themes, and sensory experiences. You use language to tell a story about their play. Narrated exploration also means using words to describe children's actions. Conversing with young children in this way helps them to develop meaning, find relationships, and create connections about the materials they are exploring. Ann Lewin-Benham, author of *Twelve Best Practices for Early Childhood Education* calls this as the art of "meaning-full conversations."

So how does one do this? First, it is important that you let children take the lead on the direction of the conversations. Do not impose or infringe on their thinking or purposefully lead the conversation in a particular direction. Let conversations unfold based on the children's perspective and not the adult's viewpoint or personal agenda.

- Expand children's play through narrated exploration, but do not interrupt their play—either verbally or physically—simply be responsive to them.

- Use descriptive words to describe materials, actions, and feelings when appropriate.

- Acknowledge children's work with words, but do not judge or critique.

(3) TRANSFORMATIONAL EXPLORATION

Transformational exploration is the aha moment when children discover the objects they are exploring can be transformed into different shapes, sizes, and textures. This type of exploration is a time of trying new ways, making mistakes, and trying again. Most importantly, transformational exploration is a time of being deeply engrossed in play without outside interference or interruption from adults.

- Promote transformational exploration with mortars and pestles along with easily crushable materials.

- Design a transformation station filled with materials for crushing, pounding, molding, sticking, and attaching.

- Create an outdoor transformation area with natural materials for poking, mixing, combining, and transporting.

BORN TO EXPERIENCE THE WORLD

Young Children are Meaning Makers

Young children are born to experience life with all of their senses. Looking out at the world with a yearning to discover the mystery surrounding them, infants and toddlers see with new eyes, hear with new ears, touch with new fingers, taste with new taste buds and feel with a new heart. Young children do not experience life like adults do. Rather, they arrive with a fresh palette of desire to meet what surrounds them and to discover what brings joy.

Young children are meaning makers. They are born with an innate and insatiable need to acquire experiences and gain understandings. When infants, toddlers, and two-year-old children actively explore and engage with their surrounding environment, they begin by making connections through day-to-day routines and experiences.

The academic-centered mindset measures a child's growth by markers and milestones not joy and wonder and strives to push children toward the next milestone whether they are ready for it or not. Yet, we know children are hardwired to learn by following their innate wants and desires to explore and discover. When teachers sidestep children's desires, we sidestep one of the most powerful forces for learning and growing.

As early childhood practitioners, how do we help our youngest children fully engage in this sensory buffet called life? One idea is to give children opportunities to play and work with natural elements because there is no greater inspiration than the gifts of nature. Fascinating objects such as pinecones, sticks, leaves, and tree pods are unassuming and open-ended. There are no specified rules or step-by-step directions on how to use them, so these natural elements invite children to bring their own hearts and minds into each experience.

Natural Materials are Meaning Makers

Natural materials are wondrous marvels, found outside your door or in natural places, and typically are free or very inexpensive. Mother Nature's palette of beautiful Natural Maker Materials encourages and inspires children's imaginations and invites them to make meaning as they experience a diverse array of shapes, textures, colors, and other fascinating elements. Natural Maker Materials delight children's senses and nourish their spirits.

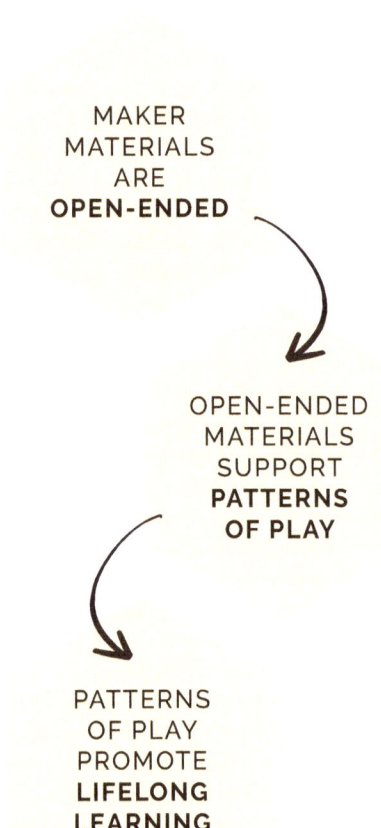

Young children are continually observing and experiencing the world through their senses; they are developing and refining what are referred to as the life senses or "will senses."[3] Although these "will senses" include the sense of well-being, sense of balance, and the sense of movement, it has been suggested that the sense of touch is one of the most important life senses. If this is true, then the type of materials children experience have the capacity to either positively or negatively impact their growth and development.

Natural Maker Materials Engage Sense of Touch. Objects and products which come from nature or are made from natural materials support and engage the sense of touch because of their inherent multiplicity of textures, sense of weight, and sense of feeling (i.e., warm or cold). Think about a simple rock. When you pick it up, the rock feels cold, but quickly warms up in your hand. The rock may appear smooth, but on closer examination with your fingers—you begin to notice ripples, indentations, and small ridges on it. It has a weight as it lies against the palm of your hand. Some rocks are heavier than others. As you discover the nuances of the rock, your sense of touch is actively engaged.

3. Hiebel, F. *Time of Decision with Rudolf Steiner: Experience and Encounter.* Hudson, NY: Anthroposophic Press, 1989.

Unlike many commercially produced toys (i.e., plastic truck or car, tea pot and cups) having a singular use or a suggested end use, Natural Maker Materials are open-ended objects and bring a variety of rich kinesthetic experiences needed to develop "will senses" in young children. Connecting children to Natural Maker Materials creates an actual and authentic connection with the gifts of Earth.

There are two types of Natural Maker Materials: (1) objects found in the natural environment or nature objects; and, (2) objects made from natural materials or natural products. Examples of objects found directly from nature include pinecones, seashells, or pieces of driftwood. Examples of objects constructed by human hands and made from natural materials include seagrass baskets, wood bowls, or wicker placemats. Both of these natural treasures pique children's curiosities because of their uniqueness.

Nature Objects. Natural Maker Materials are objects one can find in the outside natural environment. These types of materials support children's play because of their endless possibilities. As children mix, attach, detach, blend, and connect elements from nature, they learn about their physical world and how things function and work. Through the process of creating mud concoctions, for example, very young children may learn that mixing dirt with water makes mud. And, with additional amounts of water, the consistency changes into a soupy, squishy mixture. Children may also discover that adding a little paint to their concoction changes the mud's color or if the mud is painted on a stone and left out in the sun, it dries a lighter color as it hardens. They may learn that mud is cool to the touch or may discover wet thick mud sticks to tree trunks when pressed against the bark. During these simple acts of playing with mud, children learn about its properties, construct working theories, and build understandings. These thought processes, trials and errors, and problem solving skills are experiences that children will learn through the heart and carry with them a lifetime.

Natural Products. Materials that come from the Earth are called natural materials. There are inorganic materials such as stone, granite, and sand as well as native metals (i.e., copper, iron, and silver). Wood, rattan, and bamboo are biotic materials and silk, wood, and hemp are natural fibers. Natural products are made from natural materials with human hands. Examples of natural products include wood chairs or a tapestry woven from pieces of cotton cloth.

NATURE OBJECTS AND NATURAL PRODUCTS	
Nature Objects	Pinecones; Seashells; Driftwood; Tree Pods/Bark; Stones and Rocks; Dandelions; Petrified Wood; Branches with Moss; Pine Boughs; Sticks
Natural Products	Wicker/Seagrass Baskets; Wood Bowls; Woven Wood Placemats; Wood Curtain Rings; Wood Mallets; Woven Vine Balls; Popsicle Sticks; Wood Blocks

Offering young children meaningful experiences is easy when they are actively involved and given opportunities for discovering and exploring through hands-on Natural Maker Materials. With these types of materials, children are given the freedom to make choices of their own as to how the provided materials are going to be used and combined.

- Encourage young thinkers to combine Natural Maker Materials—or take them apart and put them back together again—and, to repeat the process as often as they wish. Doing this will promote the many Patterns of Play such as *Attaching & Detaching*.

- Promote discovery by placing Natural Maker Materials where children can easily access and transport them to support their play exploration needs, as well as the Pattern of Play called *Carrying & Placing*.

- Offer Natural Maker Materials in both the indoor and outdoor environments so children can expand and continue their child-led play and learning.

Storage Bins. If indoor classroom space is an issue, bins are ideal. They take up less space than sensory tables and are an inexpensive alternative. Bins are portable for use in both the outdoor and indoor environment. Low plastic storage bins, plastic wash tubs, metal wash basins, and large plastic or metal bowls can all be used in place of a sensory table.

Tips for Collecting Nature

Children are collectors. They love picking up natural objects, examining with their eyes, smelling with their noses, feeling with their hands, and sometimes tasting! As early childhood educators, our job is first and foremost to keep them safe while exploring the great outdoors. A secondary job is to protect the natural world so future generations can enjoy it. If you are planning on collecting objects from nature, here are some ideas and guidelines to get you started:

- If visiting a public park, be sure to check with the park office or ranger before collecting nature. Many parks have a "Leave No Trace" policy, which means that you must leave behind what you find for others to enjoy.

- Remember that nature does not belong to us—it belongs to the animals, forests, and flowers. So leave plenty for nature and be careful that you do not collect more than you need.

- Tree bark should be collected from the ground and not from the tree. Ripping bark from the trunk can harm the tree.

- Bring a small trash bag to carry back any generated garbage or potential litter.

- Be courteous to personal property and do not collect any natural items without permission from the owner.

Safety and Precautions for Nature Explorations

The great outdoors and all of its wonders are exciting places for infants, toddlers, and two-year-old children. For many, these places are undiscovered environments. Yet we know introducing children to the wonders of the world at a very early age can foster a lifelong love of nature. Little ones are capable, thinking beings with the innate ability to explore, and being in nature and interacting with natural elements supports their development.

To ease our fears that wee ones may injure themselves while outside—get dirt on their faces or put pieces of grass in their mouths—it helps to remember the benefits of young children having authentic experiences with nature. Although it is necessary to protect them from injury, it is also important to balance safety with opportunities for everyday encounters with the natural world. Before embarking on any indoor or outdoor nature experience, always keep safety in mind.

Here are some tips to get you started:

- Prior to playing in natural areas, conduct an inspection to assure the space is free from harmful insects, bugs, plants, and/or objects. Remove any unsafe materials; do not play in the area if there is dangerous animal life or animal feces.

- Be sure there are no toxic plants in children's play areas. Consult with local environmental authorities (i.e., landscapers or neighborhood garden shops) or the Internet for information on toxic and poisonous plants.

- Little ones explore with all of their senses, especially their mouths. Be acutely aware of any choking hazards in both the indoor and outdoor environments. Young children love to gather natural elements from the outdoors. They may fill containers with pinecones or add them to mud pie creations. Closely monitor children when exploring seed pods, nuts and pine cones because some can pose choking hazards. The choking tube is great for testing the size of an object to determine its safety.

- Be cognizant that some children may have allergies to nuts, seed pods, plants, and certain types of trees. Children with breathing disorders (i.e., asthma) may negatively react to air-borne pollen. When going outside, don't forget to bring a first aid kit that includes medications for allergic reactions (Epipens) or any other medications that need to be taken while outdoors.

- Avoid mosquito bites by getting rid of standing water. If removing standing water is impossible, use mosquito dunks, which are a safe nontoxic way to kill mosquitoes. Another way to curb mosquito and other bites is to invite wildlife that feed on insects (i.e., songbirds and frogs) into your play space. There are also insect-repelling herbs such as lemon balm, peppermint, and rosemary.

- Be aware of the possibility of ticks, which can bring disease into your play space.

- Pack drinking water to keep hydrated while out in nature.

- In wet weather, consider using puddle boots, rain capes, and waterproof outerwear to keep children dry.

- Be aware of play surfaces and always follow guidelines found in the Consumer Product Safety Commission (CPSC), *Outdoor Home Playground Safety Handbook* as well as the CPSC *Public Playground Safety Handbook*, available through www.CPSC.gov.

- Regardless of the weather, sunscreen is a must for children who are 6 months and older. The Food and Drug Administration (FDA) recommends that no sunscreen be applied to children under the age of 6 months. Children under 6 months should not be exposed to the sun between 10:00 am and 2:00 pm when ultraviolet rays are most powerful.

> Firsthand experience leads to understanding—the best antidote to fear.
>
> —Nancy Striniste

SUPPLIES FOR NATURE OUTINGS

When going on short outings with the children, the important word is "prepare." Be sure to plan ahead and bring nature outing essentials in order to make the outing as seamless as possible. With young children, always think "small." Young children's legs are short so they tire easily and quickly. Limit the time you are gone from home base. Bring a large blanket to spread out under a shade tree and take breaks to rest. Read a storybook (about nature, of course). Essential nature outings include items such as:

- Emergency Contact Information
- Diapers and Wipes
- Disposable Bags for Soiled Diapers/Trash
- Changing Pad
- Hand Sanitizer
- Snacks and Drinks
- First Aid Supplies
- Children's Medications
- Exploration Tools (i.e., Magnifying Glasses/Pails)
- Wagon to Haul Supplies or a Weary Child

PART 2

EXPLORING THROUGH
ACTIVITIES

Those who contemplate the beauty of the Earth find reserves of strength that will endure as long as life lasts.

–Rachel Carson

EXPLORING THROUGH ACTIVITIES: CHILD-LED LEARNING WITH NATURE'S BOUNTY

Through experiences with nature, young children develop an understanding of the world and an attachment to it. It's time to start exploring the great outdoors and bring the essence of curiosity and wonder into your classroom and outdoor play space.

Use the inspirations, ideas and practical tips in this section to guide and encourage even the smallest children in joyful explorations of Nature and Natural Materials.

EXCEPTIONAL EARTH p. 48

WONDROUS WATER p. 116

FANTASTIC FLORA & FAUNA p. 144

CONNECTING WITH CONCOCTIONS p. 216

EXCEPTIONAL
EARTH

Connecting with Earth

When we make direct contact or ground ourselves with the land, our bodies receive a charge from the Earth, which makes us feel better—instantly. This positive feeling may be a result of biophilia. There is a growing recognition of scientific evidence indicating young children's exposure to Earth's elements (i.e., dirt, mud, sand, clay and grass) is positively linked to psychological and emotional development, as well as more healthy and robust immune systems. Playing and digging in dirt, which most children adore, is called *grounding* or the act of connecting with the Earth.

Elemental Earthing

Give young explorers the chance to experience nature in close-up and hands-on ways. The idea of connecting children to the Earth is simple; nonetheless, babies are often confined to strollers when outdoors. Strollers impede their interactions so try leaving the stroller behind or parking it once you've reached your destination. Because this may be a new experience, it is important to be watching for cues from the children. When you place infants on the grass or ground . . . observe them . . . and talk to them as they touch, smell, listen, and look at nature.

- What did they enjoy?
- How did they interact with objects found in nature?
- What could you do to support further investigation?
- What other natural materials could you add, for them to explore?

NOTE: Some children may not like the feel of grass on their skin and express their displeasure by crying.

If this happens, gently pick up the baby and soothe him. Once the baby is calm, try placing the baby's hand on the grass or just one foot. See if you get a more positive reaction. If not, try placing a comfortable blanket between baby and the grass.

DYNAMIC DIRT

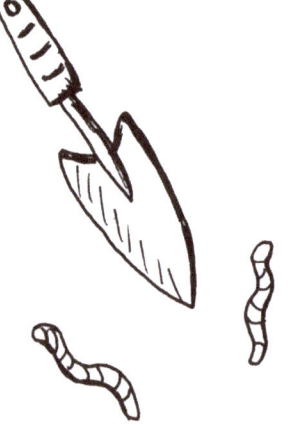

Soil, the outermost layer of the Earth, is like the Earth's skin! It's an amazing mix of minerals, air, water, and organic matter. Soil tells a story about its location and its contents reveal events of the past. But, most importantly to a child, dirt is mesmerizing. It is fun to touch, wonderful to hold, and it comes in a variety of different textures and colors that children love to explore. Dig up some dirt and watch the play begin—even a small shovelful can be fascinating and fun for young children to explore.

Dirt Detectives

Dirt bins and patches beckon little ones to dig. Simply add digging tools such as metal spoons and bowls, child-sized shovels, and small buckets. To add to the experience, secretly place plastic bugs, snakes, or worms under the soil for children to find.

Dirt Piles

Dirt piles are fascinating places for toddlers to play! They love climbing up, down, across, and over the dirt. Rolling balls down and pushing cars up the piles offers endless fun. Select a variety of "pushing" or "rolling" materials and place in a basket next to a pile of soil. Don't be surprised if there is no destination (top of pile/bottom of pile) in mind when children push or roll the trucks or cars. Children engage in Patterns of Play for the sheer enjoyment and satisfaction of movement.

DIRT EXPLORATION TOOLS			
Shovels	Buckets	Metal Spoons	Measuring Cups
Cars & Trucks	Balls	Toy Insects	Metal Bowls
Measuring Spoons	Scoops	Pots & Pans	Child-Sized Rakes

PATTERNS OF PLAY

- **HIDING & REVEALING:** When children are given opportunities to dig in the dirt, they take great delight in hiding and finding objects hidden beneath the soil.

- **PROPELLING & HINDERING:** Pushing and rolling materials up and down piles of dirt invites children to practice the *Propelling & Hindering* play pattern.

- **CARRYING & PLACING:** Dirt is a natural play material that beckons children's play pattern of transporting.

DID YOU KNOW?
Attitudes about very young children playing in a pile of dirt are mixed. Some believe that toddlers and two-year-olds should not play in dirt for fear that children will put dirt in their mouths or worse yet, swallow it. Others believe that dirt is good for the immune systems of babies.

Dr. Joel Weinstock at Tufts Medical Center found that babies who have been sheltered from dirt (i.e., bacteria) were far more likely to be sick or develop asthma, allergies, or autoimmune diseases later in life. Dr. Weinstock's research suggested excessive cleanliness interrupts the normal development of the immune system. So, what's the answer? Find a happy medium. Use the typical precautionary measures such as washing hands before eating, before and after handling food, after going to the bathroom and changing diapers, and whenever hands are dirty. But, Dr. Weinstock as well as microbiologist and immunologist Mary Ruebush maintain there is no reason why young babies shouldn't be allowed to go barefoot and play in the dirt—and, if they eat a little dirt, they are simply strengthening their immune system.

Dirt Tracks

Find a variety of small toy cars and trucks that have interesting wheel treads, place in a patch of loose soil, and watch the fun begin. Inevitably, children will swipe away the tracks with their hands—only to make more tracks again and again.

Celebrate International Mud Day (June 29th)

Founded in 2009 at the World Forum for Early Childhood Care and Education in Belfast, International Mud Day began as an exchange between the children of Nepal and Australia as a wonderful and surprising way to connect, building global understanding and relationships. It is now a celebration shared throughout the world.

MARVELOUS MUD

For many of us, when asked to recall favorite childhood memories, mud puddles and mud pies are at the top of the list. The sensory richness and open-ended play that young children experience with mud are the stuff that fabulous childhood memories are made of! With a simple touch, mud transforms; in texture, shape, and sometimes color.

PEDAGOGICAL PRACTICES
Strategies for Playing with Mud

Stage 1: Pure Exploration	*Provide a safe environment and defined area for exploring mud.* **Infants:** Put down a shower curtain under a tray of mud for exploring. Mud play can be very messy so it is best to have children in just their diapers. **Toddlers:** Fill a dishpan or bin with mud. Place outside or on a covered table for exploration. **Two's:** Build an outside mud pit complete with props for pure exploration.
Stage 2: Narrated Exploration	*Encourage conversations and naming mud characteristics.* **Infants:** Verbally describe the sensory qualities of mud. *Squishy, wet, cool, gooey, mushy, moist, sticky, oozing, brown, lumpy, slimy.* **Toddlers:** Facilitate naming the sensory qualities of mud. **Two's:** Encourage discussion about their experience of the mud.
Stage 3: Transformational Exploration	*Expand knowledge (or schemas) about mud by encouraging its manipulation in a variety of ways.* **Infants:** Include easy-to-handle cooking props (i.e., bowls, small pans) suitable for little hands. Good to have water access. **Toddlers:** Mud art and mud clay exploration in designated areas such as a kiddie pool, sensory tables, sandbox, or trays on tables. **Two's:** Mud kitchens, small mud holes in outside play space. Offer buckets, shovels, spoons, bowls, strainers, and pitchers.

Mud Paint

This makes for great outdoor painting. Mix more water than dirt to achieve a paint-like consistency. Use shallow containers to hold the mud paint, add paint brushes, and paper. For an even more interesting experience, offer large rocks for children to paint. Put a little color into the picture by adding Tempera paint to the mud. Extend the play with spray bottles of water to wash away the mud painting.

Mud Sensory Table

If you have a source of child-safe dirt outside, add some to a sensory table or bin. Add a little water to make it "mud-a-licious." Toddlers will enjoy searching for and collecting natural items to add to the sensory table such as sticks, leaves, and tree bark. Also, include toy props such as washable forest or farm animals, plastic bugs and insects, or authentic cooking props (i.e., ice cream scoop, sieve, or metal boxes with lids).

HINT
Prepare in advance for messy fun.

Put a vinyl tablecloth under the sensory table, provide vinyl smocks that cover the majority of the child's body (or strip them down to their diapers), and position a bucket of clean, warm water near the mud play for initial clean up of children's hands.

PATTERNS OF PLAY

- **HIDING & REVEALING:** Hiding a few pinecones in a pot filled with mud and then dishing up pinecone stew is great fun as children repeatedly hide and reveal or cover and uncover objects while playing.

- **CARRYING & PLACING:** Transporting, moving, and rearranging objects is serious business for young children. Offer a variety of materials and the time for children to practice the Pattern of Play of *Carrying & Placing*. Don't be surprised, however, when they transport the pots and pans to another part of the play yard!

- **MAKING & UNMAKING:** Young children quickly realize they can transform mud into a variety of shapes and sizes. As they squish, mold, mix, and crush, children are engaged in the process of *Making & Unmaking*.

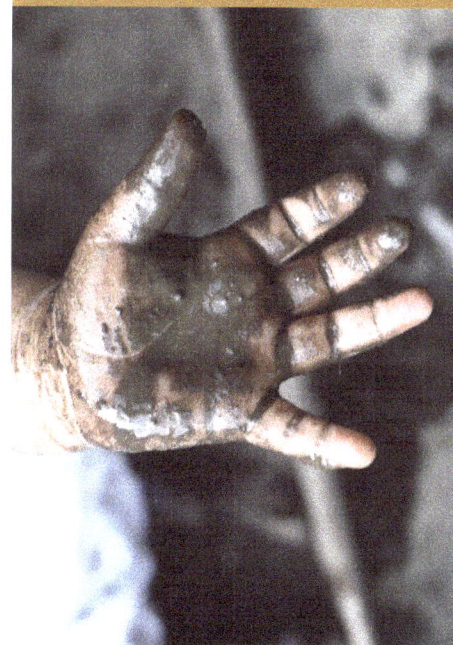

Mud Masterpieces

Gather a pile of clay-like mud. If the soil in your neighborhood isn't the right consistency, you can make mud more clay-like by adding powdered clay (found at art or construction supply stores). Invite children to dig in and make muddy sculptures. Offer natural materials (i.e., leaves and ferns) for children to incorporate into their work. Place sculptures on pieces of cardboard or tin foil and place in the sunshine to dry or support deconstruction as part of the process of play.

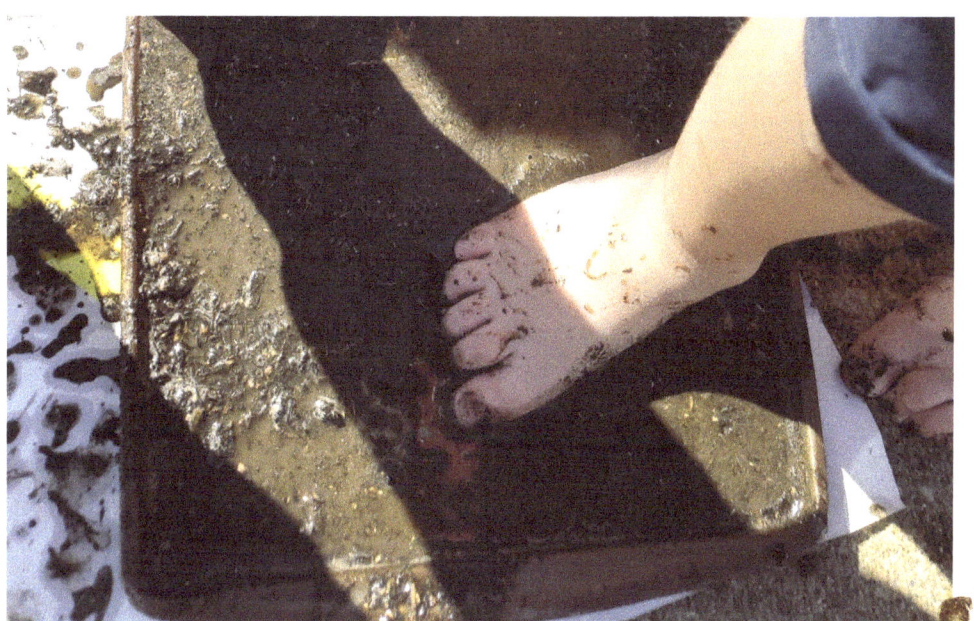

Mud Walk

Walking barefoot through mud is a wonderful sensory experience for young toddlers. After filling a low bin with mud, invite the children to hold your hand while they step in the mud and then step out onto a large piece of bulletin board paper. Continue to offer your hand for support and encourage them to walk across the paper, making footprints.

Hint: Have a second bin with soapy water for the children to step into, to help rinse off the mud. Place the soapy water bin on a large bath or beach towel to protect the bin and children from slipping. This is a great opportunity to invite parent participation.

Mud Dough

To make mud dough, invite children to help mix the following:

1 Cup of dirt
1 Cup of flour
¾ Cup of vegetable oil

Let the children stir the dry ingredients together first, then slowly add oil as the children help stir and squeeze the mixture until desired consistency is reached. Mud dough keeps in an airtight container for 7 to 10 days.

Tip: Enhance play with mud dough by placing a basket nearby with large seashells, sticks, and pinecones for children to stick in and embellish the dough.

PATTERNS OF PLAY

- **ATTACHING & DETACHING:** Playing with mud dough is a great way to practice the *Attaching & Detaching* play pattern. The experience of mud dough encourages children to connect and disconnect the satisfying, sensorial material. Children enjoy the dough while clumping together, building a pile, combining one handful with another, removing handfuls, and adding or taking away shaped pieces.

EXCEPTIONAL EARTH   63

Mud Cooking

Young children love to imitate daily life activities, especially when it comes to cooking. Along with quick access to a pile of mud, provide a variety of real life cooking props such as spoons, bowls and baking pans.

DID YOU KNOW? Offering authentic materials and props for children to use with mud encourages them to recall information from real life experiences.

This helps build memory-processing skills and encourages hand-eye coordination and the pincer grasp.

Mud Kitchens

A mud kitchen is simply a location stocked with supplies that support play with dirt, water and/or sand. It's a dedicated space for unstructured pretend play and lots of pouring, digging, measuring, and patting.

Mud kitchens come in a variety of sizes, shapes, and levels of complexity. You can purchase a mud kitchen or better yet, make your own. Thrift stores and yard sales are great places to find pieces that you can transform into an inexpensive yet very magical mud kitchen. Be creative and think outside the box when choosing repurposed furniture for children's use. For example, many types of tables (i.e., end or sofa tables) can easily convert into a mud kitchen simply by chopping down the legs to children's height. Or, if you're handy, create a mud kitchen out of scrap pieces of lumber, sanded smooth. It can be as simple or as fancy as you wish.

Just a few pieces of scrap wood assembled with concrete blocks or bricks along with a metal bowl for a sink, a few pots for cooking, and a couple of baking sheets make a wonderful place to conjure up extraordinary culinary creations from nature's dirtiest ingredients.

BASIC IDEAS FOR MUD KITCHENS		
Wagon	Small Wheelbarrow	Wading Pool
Pallets	Table	Bench
Wood Spool	Large Plastic Container	Drawer
Doors	Milk Crates	Metal Wash Tub
Tree Stumps	Cinder Blocks	Wooden Crates

AUTHENTIC COOKING PROPS FOR MUD KITCHENS

Pots/Pans/Lids	Whisks & Spatulas	Stainless Steel Bowls	Pie & Cake Tins
Baking Pans	Large Metal Spoons	Measuring Spoons & Cups	Metal Egg Beaters
Funnels	Colanders	Turkey Basters	Small Metal Coffee & Tea Pots
Woks	Muffin Tins	Ice Cream Scoops	Colanders
Plates	Serving Trays	Salt & Pepper Shakers	Mortar & Pestle

HINT
Place the mud kitchen near a vegetable or herb garden where children can find delicious-smelling herbs.

Basil, rosemary, parsley or carrot tops can be picked from the vegetable bed to stir into mud pies and cakes.

Ideas for mud kitchen transformations may include: bakery, car wash (for little cars), ice cream shop, baby bath, mud pie station, farmer's market, herb or pottery factory, pizza parlor, or whatever is meaningful to the children and their experiences.

PATTERNS OF PLAY

- MAKING & UNMAKING: Children participate in Patterns of Play as they mix, stir, swirl, and crush the mud and other natural materials while using authentic kitchen objects. Wee ones are fascinated with the transformative powers of *Making & Unmaking*.

- CARRYING & PLACING: Children earnestly engage in the Pattern of Play of *Carrying & Placing* when they gather, carry, and transport the props and materials while engaging in pretend cooking. Much of children's *Carrying & Placing* has no obvious objective and the behaviors appear to be done just for the moment and the pleasure of the moment.

Books About Mud and Mud Puddles

Puddles by Jonathan London
Puddle Pug by Kim Norman
Mud Puddle Hunting Day by Callie Grant
Brothers Are for Making Mud Pies by Harriet Ziefert
Mud by Mary Lyn Ray
Up in the Garden and Down in the Dirt by Denise Fleming

Sing a Song for Mud Pies

(Song to tune of "Sing a Song of Sixpence")
©2011 MaryAnn Kohl

Sing a song

for mud pies,

You don't

need a plan.

Mix it 'til it's mushy,

Pat it with your hand.

Put it on a pan and

Leave it in the sun.

Wait and wait

and wait a while.

Now, I think

it's done!

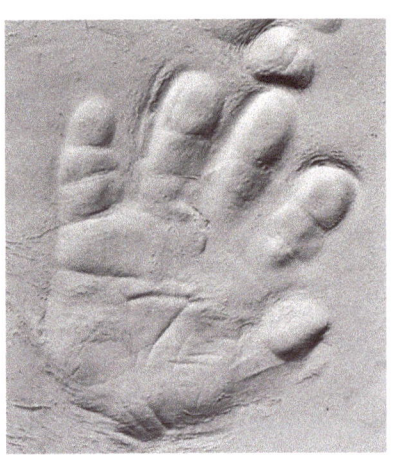

CREATIVE CLAY

Clay is an ancient earth material, composed of soil, water, minerals and other elements, formed by forces at work across time. Young children's experiences with natural clay offer a direct connection to the earth and its processes. Clay is sensory rich and offers "sense of wonder" opportunities for young children to explore changing texture, smell and pliability that is far different from typical playdough play.

EXCEPTIONAL EARTH 69

PATTERNS OF PLAY

- MAKING & UNMAKING: Children roll, pat, and construct only to smash, poke, and separate the clay when they practice the Pattern of Play of *Making & Unmaking*.

- ATTACHING & DETACHING: Children repeat transforming actions such as pulling apart and undoing immediately after they have intentionally piled, stacked, and joined the pieces of clay. With clay play, look for positioning and ordering as children place rolled balls of clay in a row or line on the work surface.

Clay is a perfect play material. It's fun to squeeze, roll, pound, poke, and squish—not only with hands, but also with feet!

Simply place a clump of clay on the floor or tabletop and let children touch, explore, and experience its uniqueness. Then, sit back and watch children's play patterns emerge.

WHY CLAY IS IMPORTANT FOR YOUNG CHILDREN

Provides Kinesthetic Experiences:
Clay offers unlimited kinesthetic discovery and hands-on experiences. It is a natural material that can be manipulated, poked, pounded, rolled, and changed.

Inspires Creativity:
Because clay is an open-ended medium, it fosters children's creativity and imagination.

Increases Attention Span:
Clay improves young children's attention span as they become engrossed with manipulating it over and over again.

Improves Manual Dexterity:
Clay improves children's manual dexterity because playing with it strengthens the pincer grasp and small muscles in the hands and wrists.

Encourages Self-Expression:
Clay encourages children's self-expression when they make decisions about its manipulation.

Enhances Emotional Growth:
Manipulating clay is a tactile experience, which is naturally soothing and calming. Social skills emerge when children talk about their creations.

Supports Communication Skills:
Playing with clay supports vocabulary and language development when children share their experiences and excitement with others.

Encourages Construction:
Clay has weight and can easily hold its shape so children's constructions have stability and will not fall apart.

Fosters Pre-Mathematical Skills:
Pre-math skills are fostered when children divide or separate large pieces of clay into small pieces.

Elevates Pre-Scientific Thinking Skills:
Clay teaches children about texture, weight, form, balance, and structure.

Promotes Problem Solving:
When children work with vertical construction (i.e., stacking and sculptures) and create 3-dimensional objects, their problem solving skills are engaged as they explore cause and effect.

Builds Self-Confidence:
Clay builds children's self-confidence because it is pliable and allows children to control and easily change the forms they make with minimal pressure of the fingers or hands.

Don't know where to begin? Does your mind conjure up thoughts of children's hands covered with clay, or the sticky clay material being stuck in the classroom carpets or rugs? Do you think the messiness of clay might be more trouble than it is worth? Here are some ideas for incorporating clay by creating an area where it's easily available for young hands:

Clay Table

Find a small, low table with edges. Tables with small drawers can hold clay tools such as rolling pins and cookie cutters. Because round tables do not have sharp edges, they work best for young ones. Cover the table in burlap or canvas cloth to keep the clay from sticking.

Clay Tray

Use a baking sheet with edges to hold the clay. Add a muffin tin for variety. Place a slightly damp cloth towel over the clay to keep it from drying out.

Clay Bin

Locate a low-sided plastic container and fill with a mound of clay. Containers with lids work well, to keep the clay from drying out. If clay does become dry, cover it with a damp cloth towel, or help children "water the clay."

Clay Board

Use a wooden cutting board for clay play. A wooden board absorbs water and cleans easily with a wet sponge. Because a clay board is a defined workspace, it helps focus young children's attention. Also, when children are encouraged to keep the clay on the board, it's easier to tidy up.

Hint: Providing children with tools like rolling pins, stamps, and mallets help them create, decorate, and shape clay pieces.

Clay Tree Stump

A large tree stump can also provide a unique surface and wonderful canvas for outdoor clay work. It's easy to clean with a hose when the activity is complete. Invite your little sculptors to press clumps of clay onto the tree trunk. Next, poke objects (i.e., stones, nuts, pinecones, small twigs, and leaves) into the clay. These items could be found under the tree, or while on a nature hunt. Encourage children to give their sculptures to the tree by leaving their work on the trunk. Sculptures will stay on the tree until the next heavy rain when they are washed away, leaving the tree ready to accept another creative gift. Because clay is from the Earth's elements, the environment is not harmed by it seeping into the ground beneath the tree.

Clay Boulder

A large boulder, especially one with an uneven surface, makes an interesting canvas for clay work. The process of pressing and peeling the clay to its surface helps young children build arm, hand and shoulder muscles. Position a large boulder in a corner of your room or in an area for outdoor play. Add clay and watch the work begin.

Clay-pressions

Fun for little ones to make, clay-pressions are impressions made in clay with natural objects (i.e., pinecones and seashells). Set out a basket of natural objects that when pressed into clay will leave a nice impression. Encourage children to flatten the clay with their hands, stomping feet, or rolling pin. Press the selected object into the clay and pull it back out. Ta-Da! A clay-pression. You might choose to let the clay-pressions air dry. After drying, children will enjoy decorating with Tempera paint or non-toxic markers.

Clay Painting

Clay can become paint by simply adding water. Inside a container, add a clump of clay and enough water to mix into a paint-like consistency. Give the children paintbrushes and a tree, sidewalk or cardboard box to paint.

Gather up treasures from a nature walk to press into clay!

TIPS FOR PLAYING WITH NATURAL CLAY

It is important to use natural or potter's clay with young children rather than modeling clay, which is oil-based. Natural or potter's clay needs frequent watering. There are two possible ways to water the clay; both are fun for little ones:

1. **Spray Bottle Method** – Show children how to make holes in the clay with their fingers or with small sticks. Squirt water into the punched holes, and cover up the watered holes with pieces of clay.

2. **Wet Paper Towel Method** – Give children a wet paper towel and show them how to squeeze out the excess water into their hands. Next, use their wet hands to water the clay. Be sure not to add too much water and remember less is more when watering the clay.

Here are some other tips for keeping clay play safe and fun:
- Remove clay residue and clean tables with a damp cloth. When dry, sanitize the tabletop.

- Provide a bin of soapy water for children to wash clay residue from their hands after use, and to avoid clogging drains with clay. When hands are mostly clean, immediately wash hands again at a sink with soap and water.

- Store clay in an airtight container to help keep the clay moist. If clay is kept out on a clay table and available to the children throughout the day, keep it covered with a damp towel and piece of plastic cloth (like a picnic tablecloth) when not in use.

- Do not use oil-based modeling clay because it may be toxic.

Clay Sculptures

Clay and nature are a great combination for creating small sculptures. Simply use the clay for sticking items together. The clay is like glue and helps to build sculptures both wide and tall. Provide a selection of items such as twigs, rocks, and shells. Let children experiment, explore, and construct.

Clay Blankets

Young children have a natural interest in making their "babies" and stuffed animals cozy and comfortable with snuggly blankets. They enjoy tucking them into bed and saying goodnight to their pretend friends. Provide a large piece of clay, small rubber mallet, and some plastic animals (i.e., bear, deer, and raccoon). Invite children to create blankets for the animals by pounding the clay into blankets and then snuggling the animals in for a quiet winter's nap. To introduce this experience, read the storybook, *Snuggle Down Deep* by Diane Ohanesian, a delightful story about fall animals nuzzling up and settling down for a wintertime nap.

PATTERNS OF PLAY

HIDING & REVEALING: When children use clay to cover an object, they are fulfilling the urge to not only cover or hide something, but also reveal the object. It is a function of enveloping and enclosing, of seeing and not seeing.

Books About Hiding & Revealing

There are several wonderful children's storybooks illustrating the Play Pattern of *Hiding & Revealing* that relate to the "Clay Blankets" experience.

Although they are written for slightly older children, the stories and realistic illustrations will capture younger children's attention.

Over and Under the Snow by Kate Messner
Over and Under the Pond by Kate Messner
Snuggle Down Deep by Diane Ohanesian
In the Small, Small Pond by Denise Fleming
UnderGROUND by Denise Fleming
Time to Sleep by Denise Fleming

Clay
By Sue Penix

I took a piece of gooey clay,

Pounded and poked it throughout the day.

I molded and formed it with my power and art,

My young child's soft and yielding heart.

I came again to play as the days went by.

I looked upon my clay and discovered it was dry!

SIMPLY SAND

Ahhh, sand! It is the quintessential fill and dump material in early childhood settings across the land. Sand satisfies a basic human need, which is why young children gravitate to it whether its location is oceanside, or between bricks in a sidewalk. There's nothing quite like the feeling of sand sifting between fingers and toes, or digging deep into a sandbox to reach the cool moist layer beneath the surface.

PEDAGOGICAL PRACTICES
Strategies for Playing with Sand

Stage 1: Pure Exploration	*Provide a safe environment for exploring sand.* **Infants:** Start with a large, flat-bottomed container with a thin layer of sand. Let little ones feel the sand between their toes and fingers. **Toddlers:** Fill a bin with sand and place it outside for exploration. **Two's:** Create a sand pit with buckets and containers for pouring and moving the sand.
Stage 2: Narrated Exploration	*Encourage naming and talking about sand.* **Infants:** Verbally describe the sensory properties of sand. *Grainy, dry, warm, gritty, loose, coarse, granular, bumpy.* **Toddlers:** Facilitate naming the sensory properties of sand. **Two's:** Encourage discussion about their experience of sand.
Stage 3: Transformational Exploration	*Encourage manipulation and play with sand in a variety of ways expanding the schema of sand and its properties.* **Infants:** Include containers and utensils for filling and spilling. **Toddlers:** Provide Kinetic Sand™, wet sand play, and sand sacks. **Two's:** Provide sand trays or sand color play.

Fill and Spill

Provide different types of authentic digging tools (i.e., large metal and wooden spoons or scoops) and dumping containers (i.e., pails, measuring cups, and tin boxes) in your outdoor sand area to encourage young children to explore the wonderful properties of sand. Or, be brave and take the sand experience into the classroom. Partially fill a hard-sided wading pool with sand, add a few digging tools, and watch the fun—and learning—begin.

EXCEPTIONAL EARTH   83

PATTERNS OF PLAY

- **HIDING & REVEALING:** Children instinctively fill, spill, and dump sand. As they dig up the sand and then immediately fill up the hole they have made, children are engaging the play pattern of *Hiding & Revealing*.

- **CARRYING & PLACING:** Children gather, dig, pick up, pour, scatter and hold as well as position and place sand. Playing with sand fulfills children's innate urge to transport materials from one place to another.

Sand Sacks

Sand sacks are a perfect way for young children to build arm strength and muscles as they tote the sacks from one place to another. Invite them to help you fill burlap rice sacks with sand. Once filled, close and secure the opening with a zip tie. Place in an outdoor open area and watch as the fun begins with children moving and dragging the sacks, climbing and jumping over them, walking on them, and taking a little rest! Inexpensive Burlap cloth sacks (12" x 14") are available for purchase online in a variety of colors.

DID YOU KNOW? Toddlers learn a great deal of scientific information by pouring and dumping the sand: gravity, measurement, mass, volume, physics, object permanence, and keen observation skills.

Other natural objects perfect for dumping and spilling include tree pods, pinecones, fresh pine boughs and large clamshells.

Sand Trays

A squiggly line here, a straight line there, and poking all around. Sand trays are a fun way to make marks in the sand. Simply provide a shallow tray lined with white paper. Coat the paper with a thin layer of sand and *Eureka!* Your sand tray is ready for little ones to draw with their fingers, hands, or a small, thick stick. Once the children are through, give the tray a shake and watch the sand smooth itself into a new surface for the next exploration.

EXCEPTIONAL EARTH

IDEAS FOR SAND TRAY SURFACES		
Pizza Boxes	Food Service Trays	Wood Trays with Sides
Plexiglass Mirrors	Box Lids	Clear Acrylic Photo Frames
Shallow Bins	Aluminum Baking Pans	Light Tables & LED Light Pads

SIGNIFICANT STONES

Rocks may be the most collected treasure of early childhood! No two are ever the same, they're found in places near and far and they're the fuel for creative, imaginative play. Small rocks fit into pockets, containers and toy trucks. Rocks are also one of the few plentiful natural materials that have significant weight. If large enough, they require muscle power to lift, carry, stack and roll. That feeling of, "I did it!" is so empowering for young children.

DID YOU KNOW?
Stonework Play is a form of creative learning. It engages the senses and animates imagination, allowing each person to tell a story or make a unique pattern suggested by handling the stones. The weight, form and texture of each stone suggest artistic choices that result in original work.

–Diane Suskind, *Stonework Play*

Reach for a Rock

Stones fascinate little ones. Why not bring these pieces of nature into the classroom? To begin, gather a few large stones, big enough to be a challenge for small children to pick up and throw, and large enough not to be a choking hazard. Choose a variety of different-colored and shaped stones that have smooth edges and dimples for visual and kinesthetic variety, such as semi-porous rocks that have all sorts of pockmarks and holes. Place the stones on the carpeted floor, sit back, and observe as the children explore these interesting objects. Think about providing containers with handles for children to put the rocks in and carry to another container.

With adult supervision, babies will enjoy exploring a little bit smaller rocks (but large enough to pass a choke tube test). Of course, infants may try exploring the rocks by mouthing them so be sure they are cleaned and sanitized before and after play.

PATTERNS OF PLAY

- CARRYING & PLACING: As children gather, carry, and hold, they notice the similarities and differences in rock color, size, and texture, so you may observe children lining up the rocks or classifying them into piles with similar characteristics.

HINT
Check out your local landscaping businesses or hardware stores for Mexican Beach Pebbles, which come in a variety of sizes and colors.

They are super smooth rocks perfect for small hands to handle and stack.

Stone Marking

Stones make an interesting canvas for children to use when painting or drawing. Use rocks or stones as an easily acquired resource for encouraging children's drawings. Stone marking is an easy open-ended activity that can take place indoors or outside.

Just follow these steps:

1. Gather stones from the local neighborhood or purchase from a garden store or nursery. Look for medium-sized stones that are large enough to pass the choke tube test but small enough for young hands to grasp. Smooth and flat-surfaced stones like the Mexican Beach Pebbles work best.

2. After gathering stones, set up a washing station with soapy water and hand brushes so children can clean the stones. Young children truly enjoy meaningful tasks and washing stones is no exception.

3. Once stones are thoroughly dry, invite children to paint the stones, or use markers to decorate them. Give children plenty of time and space to become familiar with this natural resource.

4. An alternative idea is to give the children water to paint and make marks on the stones. Marks will disappear as the stone dries.

EXCEPTIONAL EARTH 91

Stone Hideaways

Little ones love to hunt and find items in the most unusual places. Channel young children's primary urge to seek and find by playing a game of Stone Hideaways.

Preparations: Gather enough large-sized rocks for each child in your classroom. Invite the children to paint the rock their favorite color from those available (i.e., red, green, and blue). Encourage children to cover the entire rock with one color. After rocks are dry and when children are out of the classroom, spray with a sealer so the paint will not bleed onto the children's hands. Hide the stones on the playground.

Let's Play

Invite children to go on a stone hunt. Challenge the children to find all the red stones and put them in a pile or basket; then all the green stones, and all the blue stones.

PATTERNS OF PLAY

- HIDING & REVEALING: Children bury, conceal, uncover and unwrap stones that they find, to initiate this Pattern of Play. Children's pockets are also great places for *Hiding & Revealing!*

- CARRYING & PLACING: Stones are a perfect material for practicing the Pattern of Play of *Carrying & Placing*. Stones are easy to transport from here to there in children's hands as well as in different-sized containers. Providing a small wheelbarrow, wagon, or dump truck encourages many possibilities for *Carrying & Placing*.

Stone Stacking

Much like blocks, smooth flat stones make wonderful stacking materials for infants and toddlers. Stones should be smooth to the touch with no rough edges. Because river rocks are smoothed by the flow of water, they work well as stacking stones. Be sure to choose stones that do not pose a choking hazard. If the rocks fit inside a paper towel tube, they are too small to use with young children. Consider choosing stones with a little weight to them to help your little ones build muscle tone in the wrists and arms.

- Select rocks that are too heavy to throw, but light enough for two-year-olds to successfully roll and carry for short distances. Start with just one or two rocks and increase the number over time in order for children to become acclimated to the material. Rocks come in a variety of sizes, shapes, colors, and textures so there are many possibilities.

Provide adequate space for children to engage and participate in heavy moving with plenty of open space to prevent tripping over rocks. Push toys such as wagons and wheelbarrows made for toddlers can add more complexity to the experience.

Hint: Smooth River Rocks are best for stacking and can be purchased at garden shops or hardware stores.

EXCEPTIONAL EARTH

Roll a Rock

Children naturally choose repetitive play actions like pouring, sliding, or rolling things down ramps. Simply place a ramp on a slight incline with a basket of round rocks beside it. Ramps can be made from pieces of wood, PVC pipe, or sturdy cardboard.

PATTERNS OF PLAY

- PROPELLING & HINDERING: Children will work to discover how far and how fast rocks can possibly roll. They delight in finding endless ways to propel rocks such as up and down ramps, in and out of PVC pipes, and rolling on the ground while practicing the Pattern of Play of *Propelling & Hindering*.

MARK MAKING

Mark making is one of the many ways in which young children express themselves and depict the world around them. Once children can grab onto your finger, they can also hold a fat crayon or a chunky piece of chalk and begin making their mark on the world. Encourage mark making with young children by providing a variety of natural surfaces and tools for young scribes to tell their stories.

Here are some ideas to encourage mark making on a variety of surfaces with different tools.

MARK MAKING SURFACES AND TOOLS	
Mark Making Surfaces	**Mark Making Tools**
• Slate/Tile/Granite • Tree Bark* • Logs & Tree Stumps • Bricks & Cement Blocks • Sand/Clay/Mud • Sandpaper • Leaves (Large & Flat) • Cork • Large Flat Rocks/Boulders • Scrap Pieces of Wood • Burlap/Cheesecloth • Parchment Paper	• Cattails & Tempera Paint • Bamboo Pieces • Blowing Water through Reeds • Dandelion Heads & Watercolor Paint • Chalk/Watercolor Paints • Child-made Paintbrushes • Sticks and Wood Chips • Bound Group of Grass or Plant Clippings • Spray Bottles Filled with Water • Flower Heads • Large Seashells Dipped in Paint • Rattan Dipped in Paint • Ornamental Grasses

Word of Caution: Pulling bark directly from the tree can damage or possibly kill it so be sure to use only the pieces of bark found on the ground or from a fallen tree.

Mark Making on the Go

Pack a few writing or painting tools in your trail bag for children to express themselves while out and about in nature. Or, strategically place a basket of writing tools near appropriate surfaces for children to make their marks. When marking anything in nature, be sure the markings are not permanent and will be easily washed away.

Hint: Be prepared for anytime, anywhere mark making experiences. Use a fanny pack or other small tote to easily carry a few items from place to place while outdoors, for mark making. Pack a few pieces of chalk, paintbrushes, a small spray bottle of water or some watercolor paints.

DID YOU KNOW?
The process of mark making on large objects helps young ones build hand, arm, and shoulder muscles.

Mark making also encourages midline crossing. If you were to draw a line down the middle of your body, and reach your left arm over this line to touch your right ankle, you have crossed your midline.

Crossing the midline helps both hemispheres of the brain to communicate and is an important component of young children's development.

Offering experiences for cross body movement supports successful growth and development.

Spray Chalking

Children can make marks by spraying chalk on sidewalks, sand, or even snow. Making spray chalk is easy. Simply mix the following ingredients in a spray bottle:

2 Cups of water
8 Tablespoons of cornstarch
2 to 3 Drops of food coloring

PATTERNS OF PLAY

- PROPELLING & HINDERING: Children control the starting and stopping of the water spray so they are practicing the play pattern of *Propelling & Hindering*. The repetitive action of pulling the bottle's handle also allows children to construct meaning about cause and effect.

Chalk Marking

Using chalk with young children has a world of options in both the inside and outside environments. Outside, chalk works great on a variety of natural surfaces and because it is impermanent, cleanup is easy. In addition, the use of a textured surface helps to develop hand and wrist muscles needed later for actual writing. Manufacturers today must assure that chalk is non-toxic and lead free for children's use. Chalk is available in dust free varieties.

PATTERNS OF PLAY

- **MAKING & UNMAKING:** Children make marks, transform marks, and eventually wash them away by spraying or painting water onto the marks.

Here are some fun surfaces for young ones:

- **Bricks** – Real clay bricks offer interesting textures, individual bricks or on the side of a building or pathway allow for different perspectives.

- **Slate** – Unlike the typical chalkboard, recycled slate roof shingles have a wonderful textured surface for little ones to leave their scribbled chalk marks. Slate shingles are also small enough in size (approximately 9" x 12") that they can be easily transported back and forth between the inside and outside classrooms. Slate shingles can be purchased from a hardware or home improvement store and even from second chance shops that sell used construction materials at a low cost.

- **Large Rocks** – Most educators think of boulders as outside elements, but boulders can be as effective inside the classroom. Position a large rock or boulder in the corner of the classroom. Then, invite young scribes by offering colored chalk. Large boulders provide textured surfaces, which can be uneven, have crevices, and divots—all of which offer unique experiences for playing with chalk. To prevent injury, be sure the boulder is large enough that it does not roll or move.

Paint Brush Marking

Invent new mark making tools! Inspire creative thinking with natural materials and a little bit of duct or masking tape. For example, find a small stick and tape a clump of grass to the stick. Or, tape leaves to a piece of bamboo. A piece of pine bough or some dandelions taped to a small twig make interesting paint brushes, too.

- **Pine Bough Paint Brushes** – Pine boughs make perfect paint brushes. There are many species of pine trees, offering a variety of possibilities. Some have short or long needles while others have flat or bushy. Scout out different types of pines in your neighborhood. Be sure the pine boughs are long enough for children to hold comfortably. If needed, attach the boughs with duct tape to a stick in order to create a long enough handle for holding. Place Tempera paint into a container that is large enough to dip the ends of the boughs into the paint. You may want to water down the paint so it flows easily onto the paper. Dipped in paint and swiped across the paper, the pine boughs leave interesting lines and marks.

- **Dandelion Paint Brushes** – Go on a dandelion hunt and encourage children to pick several dandelion flowers with long stems. Set these out with a few containers of Tempera paint at the easel or on a table. Invite children to dip the flower head in the paint and press it on the paper.

- **Forsythia Paint Brushes** – In the spring in some regions of the United States, forsythia bushes bloom in a wonderful yellowy glory. Pick a few small stems of forsythia for children to dip in paint and swish away.

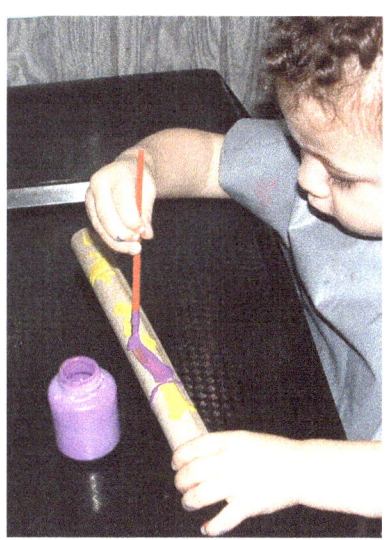

- **Bamboo Paint Brushes** – There are many ways to use a piece of bamboo for a paint brush such as dipping the end of the bamboo piece into paint and then stamping the end on a piece of paper. Children can roll the bamboo in paint and then roll onto paper (much like you would use a rolling pin). Use the bamboo stick like you would use a conventional paintbrush.

Be sure to use paint that is a little thicker so the paint will stick to the piece of bamboo.

MAGIC METAL

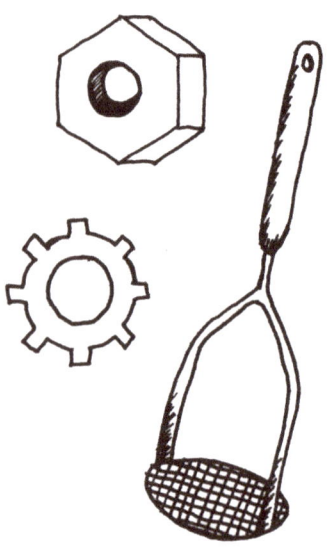

Although not immediately obvious, metal is a natural element from the earth. There are many different types of metals that are suitable for infants and toddlers to explore: copper, aluminum, iron, and silver. Each metal offers a new sensory experience for young children to discover. For example, metal is cool to the touch but warms up with children's hands. Metal has different textures and colors to explore. Most metals, especially stainless steel, have reflective qualities, which are perfect for visual stimulation of even the youngest explorers. And, one of the benefits of metal is that it is easy to disinfect due to its non-porous nature. From potato mashers to pots and pans, metals offer endless tactile experiences for infants, toddlers, and two-year-old explorers.

Metal Clay Sculptures

Metal is a perfect material to add an interesting tactile dimension to clay sculptures. Simply place metal "odds and ends" pieces (large bolts, springs, or metal bars, etc.) in a basket alongside lumps of clay and watch the creative imaginations of children as they sculpt interesting and one-of-a-kind pieces of art.

Potato Masher Prints

Scout around the resale shop and you will find a variety of potato mashers. Because the metal masher has holes in the top, it leaves unique patterns on paper. Provide your little ones with different colors of paint and a variety of different potato mashers with round and square head designs. Watch beautiful prints with intriguing patterns emerge.

Bucket Brigade

Small metal buckets are perfect for small hands and ideal for transporting and collecting natural materials while on a nature walk.

Don't forget the unique sound of natural materials being dropped into a metal bucket!

Nesting Metal Bowls

Much like nesting cups, nesting metal bowls can be stacked and placed inside each other. Infants and toddlers alike will enjoy exploring the bowls—balancing them on top of each other or fitting them inside each other.

EXCEPTIONAL EARTH   107

Assorted mirrors let children see their reflections in all different shapes and sizes!

Metal Mirrors

Infants are naturally fascinated with faces, including their own. Mirrors allow infants to explore and enjoy their reflections. While traditional glass mirrors are not safe for young children, stainless steel is a wonderful alternative. Non-breakable, with a surface shine that reflects much like a mirror, stainless steel bowls and trays make great mirrors for young children.

PERFECT PATHWAYS

Pathways offer a sense of place for young children to seek adventure, to explore, and to wonder what is just around the corner. Some pathways have destinations while others go nowhere in particular. Animals' pathways may go down to the riverside in search of water, under a briar patch for safety, or into a cave for a good night's sleep. Pathways weave in and out . . . up and over . . . over and back. Pathways guide us in our movement from one location to another. Regardless of the purpose or type of pathway, they are an important part of children's environments.

Tree Cookie Pathways

Place tree cookies in the ground for a naturally fun pathway where children can also practice their balancing skills. Make a path using a variety of different-sized tree cookies that have been cut to a variety of depths and positioned in the ground. This will challenge and enhance young children's large muscle and physical motor development.

Note: It's best to dig out a space in the ground so the tree cookie is lodged into the dirt. This will help stabilize the tree cookie and reduce the chance of tripping.

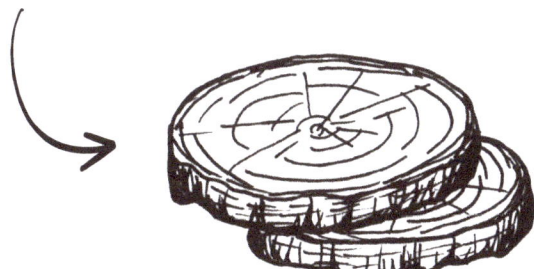

> With the first step, the number of shapes the walk might take is infinite, but then the walk begins to define itself as it goes along, though freedom remains total with each step; any tempting side road can be turned into an impulse, or any wild patch of woods can be explored. The pattern of the walk is to come true, is to be recognized, discovered.
>
> –A.R. Ammons

Circular Stone Pathways

Construct interesting pathways with garden edging stones that have been set in the ground. Stone mazes are known to calm children because it takes concentration to find their way through the twists and turns. Crying infants, for example, can be comforted simply by carrying them and speaking softly to them as you walk along the maze.

DID YOU KNOW?
It is natural for children to spin or rotate their bodies in all different directions given the opportunity. Have you ever observed a toddler spinning round and round—until even you feel dizzy? As the toddler spins through space, the cells in her inner ear are activated.

This activation sends messages throughout her entire body and contributes to the maintenance of the body's posture. This repeated behavior of *Turning & Stopping* (or spinning) contributes to the healthy development of the vestibular sense, which is necessary for young children's balance, stability, and core strength. The toddler's spinning is born out of a primary urge to change the body's perspective through movement. Promote this innate urge with circular pathways.

EXCEPTIONAL EARTH 111

Short-Grass Pathways

Did you ever play hide-and-seek in a field of wheat, garden of corn, or tall seagrass when you were young? Do you remember the excitement and anticipation you felt, waiting in just the right space for hiding from your friends? When we think about these kinds of experiences, we often think big, of sprawling fields or acres of land. Although large areas might be necessary when we are older, little ones enjoy simple groupings of plant material. All you need is a small spot with not-so-tall grass. Here are a few tips for selecting and growing ornamental grasses suitable for young children:

- Plant short-type grasses that will not grow to be too high. Children need to feel safe as they crawl or walk the pathway. You should be able to see the children from your vantage point.

- Select grasses that are soft and feathery with no sharp or jagged edges.

- If you have the space, scatter prairie grass seed over a small area. Once the grass has grown high enough, mow a path through it.

- Let a section of the lawn grow, and then mow a path through the overgrown grass.

- Add interesting objects in the pathway such as a log tunnel or slight incline to provide opportunities for crawlers as well as walkers to explore. Convex driveway mirrors laid flat in the short-grass pathway can provide interesting reflections that appear smaller on the edge of the mirror and larger in the middle, adding a new dimension for wee ones to explore.

- If you live in the land of snow, don't forget about creating winding pathways through small mounds of snow.

- Once young children become familiar with the outdoor environment, they may begin to weave their own pathways as they explore. Small wild patches with unmown grass and untrimmed bushes attract children's imaginations and attention. In many instances, children are testing their own limits and abilities as they weave in and out of the wild area. Give young children opportunities to take small risks to promote their self-confidence and autonomy.

Note: Before planting any grasses, be sure they are safe for the children in your care.

A Book About Grass

In the Tall, Tall Grass by Denise Fleming

DID YOU KNOW? Did you know that each of your feet has more than 7,000 nerve endings, making them highly sensitive and ideal for experiencing sensory stimulation?

Barfuss is a German word for barefoot. Barfuss pathways designed to stimulate the feet have been used in Germany since the 19th century.

Textured Pathways

Textured pathways are an awesome way to stimulate the nerve endings in children's feet, providing a new, creative sensory experience. Simply gather soft, gentle natural items and place them in a low cardboard box lid or trays with low sides. Place the containers on a towel or sticky mat to avoid slippage and line them up in a pathway. Be sure to put enough distance between the containers so children can easily keep their balance.

Safety Tip: Check outdoor textured pathways on a regular basis for splinters, chips, and cracks. Repair or replace parts as needed.

NATURAL MATERIALS FOR TEXTURED PATHWAYS		
Smooth Stones	Bamboo	Tree Cookies
Sand	Mud	Grasses
Hay	Flower Petals	Leaves
Pine Boughs	Tree Bark	Smooth Sticks

TIPS FOR CREATING PATHWAYS

Although the most important element of a pathway is its surface, there are other factors to consider when designing these outdoor spaces for young children:

- If space allows, create gentle and meandering curves within the path, just large enough that a small child cannot completely see around the corner. Not being able to see what's ahead creates a sense of adventure and excitement.

- Offer a variety of surfaces for visual and tactile experiences: cement, stepping-stones, wood planks, and bark, which also make unique sounds under children's feet. Use tree cookies (log slices) for stepping places for small children.

- Design pathways with surfaces that make it easy for young children (who are not quite steady on their feet) to navigate. Don't forget foot pathways could also become passages for baby buggies, tricycles, riding toys, or wheelchairs, so be sure the selected surfaces can accommodate these types of traffic.

- Position a birdhouse or bird feeder near the pathway. Get feeding instructions from the Internet, library, or a nature center.

- If possible, link the pathway to different areas of the play yard so just getting to a specific spot is an adventure in itself. If the path leads to a secret nook or hideaway, all the better!

- Include interesting objects such as bridges for children to traverse. Offer benches or places along the path for children to pause and play for awhile, before continuing down the pathway.

- Place a row of large stones or tree stumps beside the pathway for children to sit and relax.

- Add pots of aromatic flowers or an herb garden for children to enjoy nature's scents and beauty.

WONDROUS
WATER

Children love to play with water. The sound and feel of it is mesmerizing. Water offers many interesting properties for children to explore. Water lends itself to action because it invites children into unique sensory experiences when it slips across their skin, changes its shape and texture, and takes on different colors.

RAIN PUDDLES AND WATER FUN

A puddle is mysterious, inviting young children to come, look, touch, jump, and investigate: *What's that I see in the water? Wow, it looks like me! What happens when I tap the water with this stick? My goodness, it makes a splash! What happens if I use the stick like a spoon and swirl the water? Oh, the puddle has waves and bumps. What happens if I stop stirring and watch? The bumps on the water begin to disappear and the water's surface becomes smooth and silent.*

Rain puddles are outdoor science labs for young children to try out and test different theories on cause and effect. Young children test these hypotheses over and over again; just to be sure they understand the cause and effect of their stomping or tapping the water's surface. They stomp with each foot to see if the left foot has a different effect than the right foot on the water. They experiment with various types of movements such as twirling around in the water, in both directions, to see what happens. They test to see if the quickness or slowness of their stomping creates changes on the water's surface.

The next time it rains, don't sing "Rain, Rain Go Away." Pull on rubber boots, put on rain gear, and go outside to find a rain puddle!

Water Painting

Little ones love to imitate adults in many ways. Painting with authentic painting tools is a terrific strategy to help young children gain an understanding of how a paint roller and paintbrush work. Gather large paintbrushes (the larger the better), paint pans and rollers, and a little water. That's all you need for children to be in their happy place painting sidewalks, fences, brick walls, and the sides of buildings.

RAINY DAY ACTIVITIES	
Catch raindrops on your tongue	Dance in the rain
Paint with rain	Catch rain in a container
Float leaves in a puddle	Create raindrop art
Jump and splash in puddles	Sail a bark boat
Go for rainy day walk	Swirl rain puddles with a stick

What Can We Do On A Rainy/Sunny/Windy/Snowy Day?

Tune – Traditional Sea Shanty: What Do You Do with a Drunken Sailor?

By Karen Madigan

What can we do on a rainy day?
What can we do on a rainy day?
What can we do on a rainy day?
What can we do together?

What can we do on a rainy day?
What can we do on a rainy day?
What can we do on a rainy day?
What can we do together?

We can jump in rain puddles.
We can jump in rain puddles.
We can jump in rain puddles.
We can jump together.

We can catch raindrops in a bucket.
We can catch raindrops in a bucket.
We can catch raindrops in a bucket.
We can catch raindrops together.

Hint: Once the children are familiar with the song, ask what else they can do on a rainy day and then add appropriate actions to the song.

Washing Day

Wash tubs, washboards, clothesline, and soapy water create a clothes washing sensory experience for young ones to wash the doll clothes and hang them up to dry. Using large clothespins helps young children develop their pincer grasp, needed to hold a pencil for writing later on in their development. There are many other items just waiting for a good cleaning such as baby dolls, watering cans, and digging tools.

PEDAGOGICAL PRACTICES
Strategies for Playing with Water

Stage 1: Pure Exploration	*Provide a safe environment for exploring water.* **Infants:** Shallow bins to splash and explore water. **Toddlers:** Fill a bin with water and place it on the ground for exploration. Splash and stomp in rain puddles. **Two's:** Fill a sensory table with water and pouring and filling props for exploration.
Stage 2: Narrated Exploration	*Encourage naming and talking about water.* **Infants:** Verbally describe the sensory qualities of water. *Wet, liquid, clear, splash, dripping, cold, icy, tepid, warm, sparkling, soapy, dirty.* **Toddlers:** Facilitate naming the sensory qualities. **Two's:** Encourage discussion about their experience of water using words reflecting their actions.
Stage 3: Transformational Exploration	*Encourage manipulation and play with water in a variety of ways expanding the schema of water and its properties.* **Infants:** Include containers to fill and pour so children can watch the transformation of water going from one area to another. **Toddlers:** Include mild liquid soap and brushes for washing and scrubbing. **Two's:** Include funnels, pieces of hose and containers with smaller openings to fill and pour. Provide containers with Tempera paint for the children to add and mix with the water making color combinations and discovering the transformation that happens when mixing colors.

Fill 'Em Up

Fill the water table or a large, low-sided plastic container with water. In a basket next to the source of water, place a selection of plastic containers such as jugs, cups, small pitchers, bowls, and plastic bottles. Invite children to fill as many containers as they can with water. Have a mop nearby to help with the inevitable spills!

TOOLS AND MATERIALS FOR WATER PLAY

Spray Bottles	Colanders	Whisks	Watering Cans	Large Shells
River Rocks	Toy Fishing Poles	Sea Sponges	Plastic Animals	PVC Pieces
Measuring Cups	Measuring Spoons	Vegetable Oil	Leaves	Pine Boughs
Toy Boats	Water Bottles	Cups	Small Gourds	Large Corks
Plastic Tea Cups	Mild Soap	Plastic Frogs	Plastic Syringes	Food Baster
Scrub Brushes	Bars of Soap	Small Fish Nets	Ice Scrapers	Dish Cloths
Fabric Pieces	Plastic Ducks	Water Wheel	Potato Masher	Tongs
Spatula	Paintbrushes	Strawberry Baskets	Droppers	Sieves
Tea Bags	Ice Cubes	Squirt Bottles	Fresh Herbs	Funnels
Soup Ladles	Pots & Pans	Tubing	Small Sticks	Plastic Bowls

Books About Water and Rain

Water by John Hutton
Rain (Whatever the Weather) by Carol Thompson
Splash! (Baby Faces Board Book) by Roberta Grobel Intrater
The Big Umbrella by Amy June Bates

HINTS FOR SAFE WATER PLAY:

Keep a mop nearby for quick cleanup of accidental water spills.

Wear water aprons and roll up children's sleeves.

Have spare sets of clothes available for children who are extra exuberant in their play.

Keep water play tools and materials in good condition and frequently disinfect.

Whenever possible, engage in water activities outside.

Have rules for water play (i.e., Do not throw or drink water).

Use plastic containers and avoid glass containers for water play.

Be aware of any children's allergies to detergents or soaps.

Icicle Painting

Instead of knocking them down and throwing away small icicles hanging from windows, roofs and doorways, place them in a bin for the children to explore. What happens to icicles when you paint them? Place a few containers of paint with brushes next to the bin and let the children find out.

NOTE
Use caution when playing with ice to be sure it doesn't get too cold for little hands.

For safety reasons, it is important to avoid large icicles hanging from buildings, especially on a warm winter day.

Flower Ice Sculptures

Ice is one of winter's magical wonders. If you live in a cold climate area, go on an ice hunt on the playground or nearby neighborhood. Look for icicles, sheets of ice, ice chunks, or ice puddles. Encourage children's observations and discoveries by posing open-ended questions:

- What is hiding inside the ice? Can you see leaves, grass, or seeds stuck inside the ice?

- How does the ice feel? Is it beginning to melt and drip?

- What sound does ice make when it begins to melt and drip?

- What happens if you place something on the ice and push it?

- What happens if you spray colored water on the ice?

- What happens if the ice is brought into the classroom?

Freeze natural objects (i.e., fresh flowers or evergreen boughs) in small containers of water. Pop the frozen objects out of the containers and place in the water table or large low-sided plastic container. Provide food basters with warm water and encourage children to find the treasures buried in the block of ice by squeezing the warm water onto it. You could add some watering cans filled with lukewarm water to help with dissolving the ice.

SQUISHY SEA SPONGES

Straight from the ocean, natural sponges are an intriguing art material for little ones. They come in a variety of shapes and sizes and are full of nooks and crannies, making them ideal for creating interesting and beautiful pieces of art with texture and unique designs. Sponges are also a fun material to play and experiment with on a hot summer day by adding them to water play.

Sponge Squeeze

Provide a small plastic bowl or tray, partially filled with water, along with a dry sponge. Wee ones instinctively grab for the sponge and dump it into the water. This is a perfect experience for even the youngest child.

PATTERNS OF PLAY

- **HIDING & REVEALING:** As wee ones experiment with a sponge and water, they are involved in the hiding of water (in the sponge) and the revealing of water when they squeeze the water out of the sponge. Children are also watching the transformation of the sponge as it goes from dry to wet.

HINT
Using natural sea sponges for children's play is a wise choice:

1. Natural sponges do not have any of the potentially harmful chemicals found in man-made sponges.

2. Bacteria can be eliminated in natural sponges because they are easier to clean compared to man-made sponges.

3. Natural sea sponges are eco-friendly and biodegradable.

Squishing sponges is a great exercise in cause and effect.

Sponge Walk

Place two buckets or bowls a short distance from each other. Fill one with water colored with food coloring, about two thirds full. Keep the second bowl empty. Place some dry sponges next to the bucket with the colored water. Encourage toddlers to soak up the water with the dry sponge, walk over to the empty bowl or bucket, and squeeze the water from the sponge into the empty bucket.

PATTERNS OF PLAY

- CARRYING & PLACING: Children experiment with moving the water-filled sponge back and forth, and repetitive squeezing as they "make" and "unmake" the water in the sponge. Be prepared for a watery mess. This activity is best done outside because the water-laden sponge will drip everywhere—including on the children's clothes.

Sponge Splatter

Sponge splatter painting is a fun outdoor activity done with just water or possibly Tempera paint. For the painting experience, place a large piece of cloth, old bed sheet, recycled tablecloth or canvas on the ground. Place several shallow containers of paint with sponges nearby. Invite children to dip the sponges into the paint and drop on the canvas, creating a splatter painting. Consider using different textured sponges with a variety of paint colors. Young children enjoy painting with sea sponges, and they will love listening to the sound the sponge makes as it "splats" on the paper. After the cloth has dried in the sun, hang the fabric in the room for decor or create a tent for dramatic play experiences.

Safety Tip: Check natural sponges often for tattering and replace when needed.

BEAUTIFUL BUBBLES

Babies absolutely love bubbles. So, if there's one thing you always want to have on hand whenever the need arises, it's bubbles! No teacher of little ones should ever be caught bubble-less. Bubble-watching is a fun activity for infants, chasing bubbles is great for toddlers, and playing with bubbles is a terrific learning activity for two-year-old children.

PEDAGOGICAL PRACTICES
Strategies for Playing with Bubbles

Stage 1: Pure Exploration	*Provide a safe environment for exploring bubbles.* **Infants:** Blow bubbles for babies to watch. **Toddlers:** Blow bubbles for toddlers to catch and chase. **Two's:** Provide bubble wands for children to blow bubbles.
Stage 2: Narrated Exploration	*Encourage naming and talking about bubbles.* **Infants:** Verbally describe the sensory characteristics of bubbles such as wet, soapy, float, round, pop, shiny, sparkling. **Toddlers:** Facilitate the naming of the sensory characteristics. **Two's:** Encourage conversations about the bubble blowing experience.
Stage 3: Transformational Exploration	*Encourage manipulation and play with bubbles in a variety of ways, expanding the schema of bubbles and their properties.* **Infants:** Place water in a shallow, non-breakable container to feel, splash, and explore. **Toddlers:** Include wire whisks to whip up bubbles in a soapy mixture. **Two's:** Include paint to transform bubbly, soapy water into a colorful mixture for printing with simple objects.

DID YOU KNOW? Not only is chasing a bubble a great way to promote gross motor skills, it helps children develop proprioception.

Proprioception is the child's unconscious perception of movement through space as well as the orientation of their body in space. Very young children are just beginning to develop proprioception so they are learning where their hands and fingertips end and where the objects they are reaching for begin.

PATTERNS OF PLAY

- **TURNING & STOPPING:** Children twist and turn as they are moving their bodies to get close to the floating bubble. Once children reach the bubble, they may come to an abrupt halt as they pop the bubble.

Beautiful Bubble Recipe

Don't have time to go to the store and purchase a bottle of bubbles? Don't worry, bubbles are easy to make at home or in the classroom.

Best bubble recipe ever:

2 Cups water (distilled water is best)
½ Cup blue Dawn® dishwashing detergent
¼ Cup glycerin (found in pharmacy store)

Stir the three ingredients together, trying not to create soap foam. Pour the mixture into a plastic container with a lid and store overnight. When ready to use, gently stir and pour bubble mixture into a low, flat-sided container. Dip a bubble wand into the mixture and blow!

Caution: Very young children may not understand the difference between inhaling and exhaling, or blowing the bubbles. It's important to approach bubble blowing in a slow, safe way, which may mean one-on-one time with an adult and child. Blowing bubbles is definitely an experience for the older two's but not for any younger child.

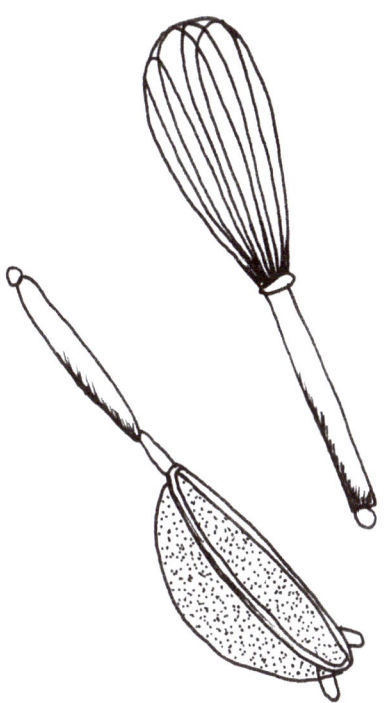

Kitchen tools make great bubble blowers.

EVERYDAY OBJECTS FOR BUBBLE BLOWING

Spools	Colanders	Pipe Cleaners
Towel Rolls	Short Pieces of Tubing	Bamboo
Mesh Fabric	Small Sieves	Coated Wire

Whisking Bubbles

Place a container of water on the ground and add a mild soap solution. Provide a variety of whisks for the children to beat the solution to make bubbles.

PATTERNS OF PLAY

- MAKING & UNMAKING: Children beat the solution to make the bubbles appear and then make them disappear when they pop the bubbles with their hands.

Bubble Painting

Mix Tempera paint and a few drops of non-toxic dish soap in a small bowl. Add water to the container to create a rather thin liquid. Using a whisk or hand crank beater, make bubbles in the container until they rise to the top of it. Hold a white piece of paper over the bowl. The bubbles will explode on the paper, creating a bubble print.

Note: Children enjoy cranking the hand beater, but be sure to exercise safety measures to prevent pinched fingers.

Bubble Bubble

By Sue Penix

Bubble, Bubble
Float Up High.

Bubble, Bubble
Touch the Sky.

Bubble, Bubble
Turn Around.

Bubble, Bubble
Touch the Ground.

Bubble, Bubble
Stop, Stop, Stop.

Bubble, Bubble
Pop, Pop, Pop!

SPECIAL SEASHELLS

Seashells are gifts from the sea. They come in all shapes, sizes, and colors and are wonderful natural objects for young ones to discover and explore. With a variety of textures (smooth, bumpy, pointy), seashells offer abundant sensorial experiences for young children. And no two seashells are exactly the same.

Seashell Sounds

Provide a variety of cone-shaped and medium-sized shells. Encourage children to hold the shell up to their ear and listen to the sounds resonating inside the shell. Seashells make a tinkling sound when placed in a metal or wooden bowl and swirled around. Provide a variety of props such as large metal or wooden spoons or perhaps a whisk for stirring seashells in containers.

Note: Before offering any seashells to wee ones, be sure they pass the choke tube test, or cannot pass through a paper towel tube.

Stringing Seashells

Many seashells have natural holes and make ideal stringing objects. Offer these kinds of seashells with shoelaces (the thicker and bigger the better) at a small table for toddlers to explore.

All in a Row

Toddlers enjoy lining items up end to end, moving them, and lining them up again. Seashells are a perfect natural medium for this kind of play. Provide a basket filled with a variety of medium-sized shells in different colors, shapes and sizes. Sit back and observe how the children explore, line up, or bunch the shells together.

PATTERNS OF PLAY

- CARRYING & PLACING: Children may also wish to carry the seashells from one place to another, so try providing containers to support their explorations.

- PROPELLING & HINDERING: Children submerge and move seashells and other objects in water. They are especially fascinated with how their hands and objects move through and under water.

Clamshell Painting

Clamshells can be a wonderful canvas for little ones to paint and are readily available at craft stores or better yet, pluck them from the ocean if you live near the shore. Provide a paintbrush or sponge to paint the clamshell with Tempera paint or watercolors. Add liquid glue to help the paint adhere to the shells. A large clamshell also makes a wonderful "sea plate" or water scoop to add to the mud kitchen.

Note: Examine the edges of the clamshell, and run your fingers around the edge, to be sure it is safe, before giving it to the child.

Seashell Small World

Partially fill a small low-sided container. Place a basket of several medium-sized seashells, natural sponges, and toy sea creatures nearby, for your little ones to explore creating a mini ocean habitat.

FANTASTIC FLORA & FAUNA

Nature always wears the colors of the Spirit.
—Ralph Waldo Emerson

Introduce young children to the delights of animal, insect and plant life, from small dandelions growing wildly in a sidewalk crack, to grand trees growing majestically in your backyard or neighborhood. For young children these everyday plants, flowers, and trees are marvelously new and waiting to be explored. When children do, they delight in finding the chipmunks, birds, bees, squirrels, ants, butterflies, and worms that call the plants "home."

LOFTY LEAVES

Young ones may not understand why trees drop their leaves in the autumn, but they are completely fascinated by the sounds the leaves make when walking through them. They delight in picking up leaves, tossing them in the air, and watching as they float back to the ground. When crumbling and crunching autumn leaves with hands or feet, young children discover different textures, smells, and sounds. Create opportunities for little ones to crawl, run, kick, roll, toss, and sit among the leaves. In doing so, you are strengthening children's large motor skills, enhancing tactile experiences, and providing unlimited amounts of joy.

Catch a Leaf

Leaves gently falling from trees beckon both young and old to come and play "catch me if you can." Watch for a day when the trees are shedding many of their leaves . . . usually on a day with a gentle breeze . . . go outside . . . catch a leaf or two. Dance around the tree with your leaf and welcome autumn to the neighborhood.

DID YOU KNOW? The senses (smells, sights, sounds, tastes and feels) work together to help children process information about the world around them.

The more the senses are activated, the more children learn. Sensory integration takes place as the brain processes and receives sensory information, organizes it, and responds appropriately. Play experiences outdoors with natural materials engage the senses—sometimes all of them at once.

Classroom Fun with Leaves

Leaves in the great outdoors are the best but bringing leaves inside the classroom is also very fun. Here are some ideas to try:

- Fill a large low-sided cardboard box with autumn leaves of various colors, shapes, and sizes. Encourage children to get into the box and explore. If you work with the smallest of children, help them into the box and sit beside it. If the box is large enough, get into the box and play with the child. Under your watchful eyes, children's explorations might even reveal hidden insects, soil, or bits of decomposing branches or leaves.

- Find a low-sided plastic container and fill halfway with lukewarm water. Add autumn leaves and encourage the children to play, noticing which items float or sink. Add large rocks, wet leaves will stick to them!

- String large autumn leaves on short pieces of string. Hold the threaded leaves in front of the infant and encourage him to pull off the leaves. Since autumn leaves are very fragile, this is an easy yet fun experience where children learn about their own power with cause and effect.

- Be on the lookout for extra-large autumn leaves (i.e., sycamore, maple, etc.) for children to paint. Dab a bit of finger paint on the leaf and encourage little ones to spread the paint around with their fingers . . . and even toes!

- Make an autumn collage with paper, glue, and leaves that toddlers have found on a nature walk. Provide a tray for the activity to accommodate enthusiastic gluing.

- Invite parents and 2-year-olds to bring in a large autumn leaf from their backyard or neighborhood. Set up a place in the classroom where the leaves can be displayed, touched, and enjoyed.

Leaf

By Karen Madigan

Find a leaf on the ground.

Pick it up and twirl around.

Tap your head, tap your knee.

Kiss your leaf, and now kiss me!

Note: Use an authentic leaf and act out the poem's words to promote language and physical skills.

Leaf Angels

Just like making angels in the snow, it's fun to make leaf angels in crunchy, earthy-smelling leaves. Making leaf angels is a total sensory integration experience using the whole body!

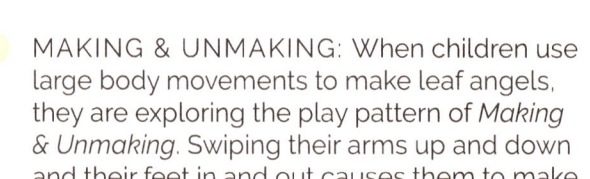

PATTERNS OF PLAY

- MAKING & UNMAKING: When children use large body movements to make leaf angels, they are exploring the play pattern of *Making & Unmaking*. Swiping their arms up and down and their feet in and out causes them to make and unmake a full body shape.

Leaf Transporting

Toddlers need big and meaningful work, especially work that involves transporting things from one place to another. Provide size-appropriate wheelbarrows, wagons and other large containers for children to fill and move from one location to another. This transporting experience fills the senses with the smell of the earth, and the sound and feeling of rustling, crunchy leaves. It also supports the development of large and small muscles, hand-eye coordination, manual dexterity, and balance.

PATTERNS OF PLAY

- CARRYING & PLACING: Children fill, dump, and transport containers of leaves as they carry the autumn gems from one place to another.

TRANSPORTING TOOLS		
Child-size Wheelbarrow	Paper Grocery Bag	Picnic Basket
Old Suitcase	Roller-Bag	Shopping Bag
Child-size Wagon	Plastic Gallon Milk Jugs	Watering Can

Leaf Marking

Children love to paint. Instead of painting on paper, provide an alternative material such as a large leaf. Examples of large leaves include broad-leaved silver birch, catalpa, and magnolia. Smaller leaves can be painted, placed under a sheet of paper, and pressed to create beautiful leaf prints.

Leaf Prints

This is a great activity for older toddlers. After children enjoy finding leaves, place them under a piece of thin muslin fabric and invite children to pound the fabric with a rubber or wooden mallet. The leaves will release their color into the thin fabric. Green or freshly fallen leaves work best.

Autumn Hunt

Fall leaves make a wonderful blanket to hide fun objects. Simply hide selected objects in leaves and let the children toddle through the leaves as they hunt. You may observe children finding the object and then replacing it and covering it again with more leaves. Here are some ideas for objects to hide:

- **Gourds and Mini-Pumpkins** – Autumn gourds come in a variety of shapes, sizes, and textures and make perfect objects for a hide-and-seek game. Count the objects before you hide them so you can be sure to retrieve all of them. If not, gourds or mini-pumpkins will make tasty snacks for visiting creatures.

- **Plastic Eggs** – Prior to the hunt, fill the eggs with a variety of objects (i.e., bells, rice, small stones, and beads) and glue the eggs together so they will not come apart. Hide the eggs among piles of leaves, for hunting. Once all the eggs are found, play a shaking game to hear the different sounds of the eggs.

PATTERNS OF PLAY

- HIDING & REVEALING: Children find and hide objects in piles of leaves as they innately dig, move about, or throw them into the air. In addition to the play pattern of *Hiding & Revealing*, young children are also engaging in viewing the leaves from different perspectives and orientations (on the ground or in the air). When children lie on the ground and cover themselves up with leaves, they are practicing the play pattern of *Enveloping & Enclosing*.

Sunny Leaf Catchers

Sunny leaf catchers are easy for even the youngest child to make. The sun shines brightly on the leaves and children enjoy the unique patterns and colorations. All you need is clear contact paper and collected leaves. Cut the contact paper to the desired length (approximately 24" square). Tape to a flat surface, with the sticky side out, and invite your little ones to place leaves on the contact paper. When the children are done, seal the leaves with another piece of contact paper. Display on a window or glass door, making sure it is low enough for children to enjoy. If there are no windows or a glass door in your classroom, try placing the sun catcher on top of a light table for children to explore.

This is a fun expedition for two-year-olds who can walk and search.

Crunchy Crunch

Search for leaves that are dried, crunchy, and brown-colored. Invite children to rip the brittle leaves into small pieces. After placing a few small pieces in the bottom of a mortar, encourage children to use the pestle and begin grinding by firmly pressing the pestle to the bottom and sides of the bowl in order to crush the leaves. Continue the crushing and crunching. If done long enough, the leaves will turn to a fine powder.

A mortar and pestle are valuable hands-on learning tools. When children repeat the action of pressing and twisting the pestle, they are challenging their bodies to repeat, repeat, and repeat again. In addition to fulfilling the need for doing and undoing, they are also building body strength. The arms, upper back, chest, and shoulders are all strengthened while crushing leaves with a mortar and pestle.

If you are unfamiliar with a mortar and pestle but want to try them out, here are a few tips for finding the right one for your classroom:

- Round shaped mortars work best.

- Choose a large pestle with a big head for best grinding results.

- Be sure the pestle is the right length. Too short causes children to bump their hands on the mortar and too long results in not as much pressure being used.

- Although mortar and pestles come in a variety of materials (wood, granite, marble, ceramic, stone), the best one for ultimate grinding success is the Mexican version called the molcajete. If concerned about breakage, select a wooden mortar and pestle but do not expect the same grinding results as stone or granite.

PATTERNS OF PLAY

- MAKING & UNMAKING: Children's repeated actions of grinding leaves with the mortar and pestle offers opportunities in the play pattern of *Making & Unmaking*.

Books About Autumn Leaves

Fall Leaves by Liesbet Slegers
Fall (Bright Baby Touch and Feel) by Roger Priddy
I Love Fall! (A Touch-and-Feel Board Book) by Alison Inches
Baby Loves Fall!: A Karen Katz Lift-The-Flap Book by Karen Katz
Fall is Here! by Fhiona Galloway

Leaves
By Sue Penix

(REPEAT x1) The leaves come tumbling down
(Wave a leaf in a downward motion)
All around the town
(Spin around)
The leaves come tumbling down
(Wave a leaf in a downward motion)

(REPEAT x1) Pick a leaf and turn around
(Hold a leaf and turn around)
Turn round and round
(Spin around)
Pick a leaf and turn around
(Hold a leaf and turn around)

TREMENDOUS TREES

Trees play a vital role in the natural world. They are valuable resources used by both animals and humans. Trees give us the gift of oxygen and clean air. They offer shade, shelter, and provide food. Trees prevent soil erosion and the Earth's groundwater is filtered through their roots. Research has shown that certain types of trees have an impact on reducing crime in urban areas and increasing healing for hospital patients with window views.[4] Trees provide countless hours of joy for children. Little ones love to feel all that trees offer: bark, leaves, twigs, and seed pods and babies enjoy napping under the shade of a tree's leafy boughs. Active two-year-old children find themselves hugging tree trunks, running around and around trees, and even attempting to climb!

Gifts to Trees

The majestic tree standing tall inspires children's awe and wonder. Young children are drawn to trees. Perhaps the attraction is because trees are so much bigger than they are. Maybe it's because even the youngest child can intuitively feel and sense the tree's strength and power. Adopt a nearby tree and make frequent visits. Greet the tree with a hug or a "thank you for being here" song. Personalize visits even more by having children offer a gift of gratitude or thanks. Examples of child-made gifts include decorated pinecones, recycled lid chimes, or child-made birdhouses.

> Give thanks for what you have been given. Give a gift, in reciprocity for what you have taken. Sustain the ones who sustain you, and the earth will last forever.
>
> —Robin Wall Kimmerer

[4] Donovan, G. & Prestemon, J. "The Effect of Trees on Crime in Portland, Oregon." *Environment and Behavior,* 44(1), 3-30, 2012.

Tree Bark Marking

Tree bark makes a perfect canvas for young children's artwork and is an interesting alternative to paper because of its texture and bumpiness. Tree trunks offer a great vertical surface providing sensory opportunities for children. Good mark making tools include chalk, charcoal, or anything that will wash away with the next rain. You can also use loose tree bark for mark making. Scout around for bark that has fallen to the ground. Be sure not to pull bark directly from the tree because doing so could damage or possibly kill it.

Tree Peek-a-Boo

One of the first games young children learn to play is Peek-a-Boo. Little ones love to hide behind things, including trees, and peek around the trunk to see who is watching.

PATTERNS OF PLAY

- HIDING & REVEALING: Children repeat actions to hide behind the tree trunk then reveal themselves or watch as another person takes on the hiding/revealing role.

While they are playing the game of Peek-a-Boo, they are touching and feeling the tree's trunk discovering its texture, and nooks and crannies in the bark.

Tree Cookies

Tree cookies are slices of tree branches. Typically the size of a real cookie, they can be a variety of sizes, from small to very large. Sometimes the very, very large tree cookies are lovingly called "tree cakes." Tree cookies can be purchased online or from catalogs, they are also easy and economical to make. After a heavy rainstorm, look around the neighborhood for fallen branches. Hardwoods like cherry, oak, and maple work well and tend to last longer than softwoods. Be sure to select branches that are free of molds, decay, and insects and are at least 2" in diameter. Once you've found a tree branch, simply cut it with a hacksaw or hand saw into slices (or cookies) at least ½-inch thick. Sand slices, place the slices on a cookie sheet and bake them for 15 minutes on the lowest oven setting. This will season the wood and kill any bacteria that may be present. Another option is to soak the cut tree cookies in a bucket of mild bleach water overnight. Be sure to check them on a regular basis for chipping, cracking, and splinters and to replace them as necessary, to prevent injury.

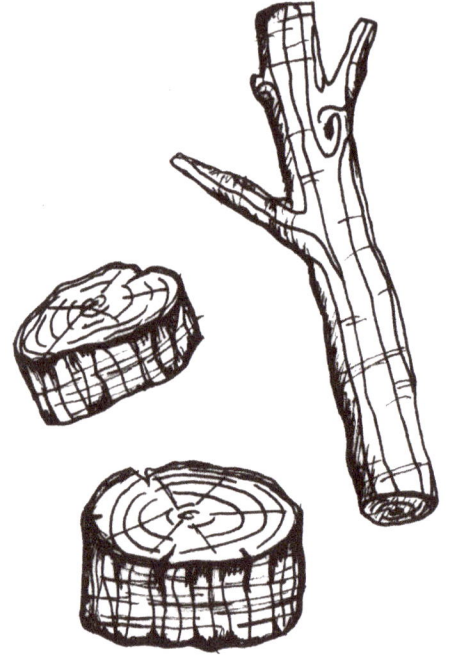

Tree cookies are extremely versatile and used in multiple places around the classroom. They can become a multitude of imaginary props such as boats, tables, chairs, and meatballs for the pretend soup. Here are some additional ways to incorporate tree cookies into day-to-day experiences with young children.

- **Tree Cookie Sorting** – Provide tree cookies for little ones to stack and sort. Add a variety of containers with compartments such as muffin tins, wooden bowls, and trays. Offer children opportunities for creating their own colorful tree cookies for stacking and sorting. Provide paint, markers, or crayons and watch the creativity begin.

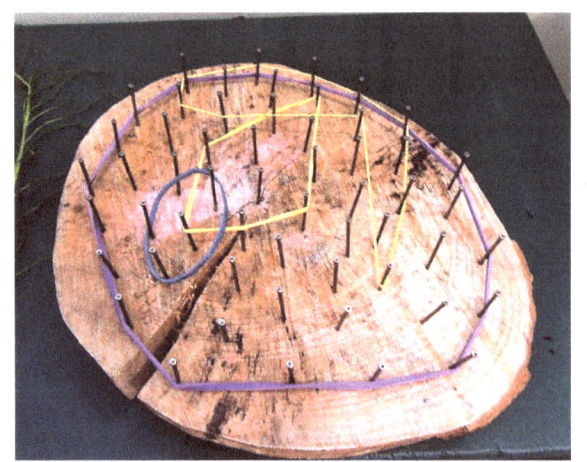

FANTASTIC FLORA & FAUNA   165

- **Tree Cookie Lacing** – Young children will enjoy making colorful designs with multiple-colored shoestrings as they lace the strings in and out of the holes of a tree cookie. To make a lacing cookie, choose a branch slice that is approximately 5" to 6" round and 1" thick. Drill holes all the way through the cookie that are approximately ½" to 1" in diameter. Sand the surface and edges of the holes. Use large, thick shoestrings for lacings. Work boot shoelaces make terrific lacings for tree cookies. Invite the children to lace by simply placing a few different-colored shoestrings in a basket next to the tree cookie. Offer a little novelty to children's lacing with long-stemmed dandelions or pliable and narrow sticks for the children to thread a tree cookie.

PATTERNS OF PLAY

- ATTACHING & DETACHING: Children weave shoelaces in and out of the tree cookie to attach the laces to it. Then, when they take the shoelace off the cookie, they are experiencing the play pattern called detaching.

Books About Trees

On My Leaf by Sara Gillingham

Babies in the Forest by Ginger Swift

Forest Baby by Laurie Elmquist

DID YOU KNOW? Lacing has many benefits for the two-year-old. Stringing objects strengthens bilateral coordination, which is the skill of using both hands simultaneously.

We frequently use this skill in everyday activities such as tying our shoes, typing on the computer, and buttoning our clothing. Lacing also helps in the development of fine motor skills and hand-eye coordination.

BOUNTIFUL BIRDS

The graceful eagle swooping through the blue sky, red-headed woodpecker tapping on the tree, or a pair of chickadees flitting about the yard all create a visual feast for children and adults alike. Researchers such as Ratcliffe, Gatersleben, and Sowden, have found a significant positive connection between listening to bird sounds, attention restoration, and stress recovery. Experts from Portland Audubon believe that bird watching for adults is mesmerizing, producing a calming and positive emotional effect on our bodies and minds. In addition to a calming effect, bird watching also helps us focus, watch, and listen. The same may be true for young children. Consider these additional benefits watching birds might have on infants, toddlers, and two-year-olds:

BENEFITS OF WATCHING BIRDS		
Infants (8+ Months)	Toddlers	Two-Year-Olds
Eye Tracking Tracking moving objects helps develop eye movement and subsequent hand-eye coordination.	**Object Recognition** Watching birds helps children recognize and begin to distinguish them from other creatures such as squirrels.	**Vocabulary Development** Observing birds increases children's vocabulary and naming of flying objects (i.e., bird, butterfly).

Inviting Birds to Visit

There are many ways to invite birds into your neighborhood, either by the classroom window, in the play yard, or in the nearby vicinity. Three important elements are necessary to attract birds: food, water, and a safe habitat.

> No child should grow up unaware of the dawn chorus of the birds in spring . . . In that dawn chorus, one hears the throb of life itself.
>
> —Rachel Carson

ELEMENTS FOR ATTRACTING BIRDS

Food	Water	Habitat
Plant/Tree/Flower Variety • Berries • Seeds • Fruits • Nuts • Nectar **Feeding Stations** • Platforms for ground feeders • Hanging for perching birds • Suet for insect eaters	**Water Sources** • Birdbaths • Drippers • Misters • Flowing or circulating water • Sprinklers • Hummingbird feeder • Puddles	**Foliage Height Variety** • Ground cover (2" high) • Shrubs (4' to 10') • Small trees (6' to 15') • Tall trees (15'+) **Shelter** • Nesting materials • Nesting houses/bird houses • Safe/protected • Appropriate size/location

Bird Feeders

Even the youngest child can help create places birds can call home. Start by finding out what a bird needs. Bluebirds, for example, are shy so they prefer their homes facing open spaces or lawns with little tree cover. Chickadees, on the other hand, prefer their home facing fields of flowers and are happiest with some tree cover or shrubs for security.

The size of the birdhouse, entry hole size, and even where the house is located are important in attracting birds to your neighborhood. Generally speaking, birds need freedom from predators, adequate food and water, and shelter from nature's elements. When purchasing or constructing a birdhouse,

FANTASTIC FLORA & FAUNA   169

pay attention to the size of the entry hole. If it is too big, it invites predators (i.e., mice and possums) as well as other species of birds that will raid the nest and have an egg for lunch. Snakes will also invite themselves into the bird's home for an egg snack if the birdhouse is positioned low to the ground.

Although most birdhouses are placed in trees, a preferable and safer location is a simple post several feet off the ground. Most birds prefer a perch or landing edge just outside the entry hole. They also need a constant and reliable source of water such as a water fountain or birdbath.

Check with local experts to decide which birds you would like to attract to your space.

Hummingbird Heaven

If you live in a region where hummingbirds locate, spice up your outdoor classroom for the world's smallest bird, the hummingbird. Hummingbirds are naturally attracted to bright colors, especially the color red because many of the flowers they drink nectar from are red in color. If you want to attract hummingbirds, here are a few tips.

1. Plant native plants and flowers that attract hummingbirds. As a bonus you'll attract butterflies too as they enjoy many of the same flowers. Include flowers such as columbine, cardinal flowers, and daylilies. Check with your local garden shop for native plants that attract hummingbirds. Plan your garden so you have flowers blooming throughout the birds' entire migration period.

2. Plant some of the flowers under a classroom window so children can observe the hummingbirds from the window.

3. Place feeders out mid-March through October. Southern states can leave feeders out year-round as more and more hummingbirds are wintering in the United States.

4. Keep feeders clean and change food every week.

5. Tie a red or orange ribbon around a tree or in a bush in your play yard, and hang a feeder in the tree or bush. The more red and orange a hummingbird sees, the more likely they are to stop by your feeder and continue to visit.

6. Have the children make red ornaments from plastic lids to hang in the outdoor classroom near your hummingbird feeder.

Hummingbirds are attracted to bright colors, especially red!

Hummingbird Food

You can make hummingbird food using this easy recipe: 4 parts water to 1 part sugar (regular white cane sugar). Do not use honey or brown sugar, as these types of sugar are not good for the hummingbird. Red food coloring should not be added to the water because it is harmful to hummingbirds. To make delicious hummingbird food, heat water and sugar mixture on the stovetop until it comes to a boil. Remove from heat and let cool to room temperature before placing in the feeder.

Bird Nest Discovery Bin

Place shredded paper, grass clippings, twigs, plastic eggs, and toy birds in a low bin on the floor. Invite the children to explore the materials and practice constructing and deconstructing bird nests. Place a few laminated pictures of authentic birds and nests next to the bin for added interest and conversations.

PATTERNS OF PLAY

- **HIDING & REVEALING:** When children play with the bird nest discovery bin, they practice hiding and revealing of the birds in the shredded paper or other nest materials.

- **MAKING & UNMAKING:** Children explore materials while choosing items to "weave" together and take apart while building a bird nest.

Nesting Gifts

Attract birds to your backyard by offering gifts of materials they can use when constructing their nests. Fill a strawberry basket or mesh bag (i.e. potato or onion bag) with the materials that birds need to build their nests. Examples of materials include small pieces of ribbon, yarn, string or fabric, dryer lint, milkweed down, raffia, and cotton balls. Hang the filled basket or bag in a spot where the contents can stay dry and out of reach of animals such as squirrels or cats. A perfect place for hanging is where children can observe the birds selecting and tugging out the nest gifts.

Books About Birds and Nests

Baby's First Book of Birds and Colors by Phyllis Limbacher Tildes
Nest by Jorey Hurley
Flip, Flap, Fly! A Book for Babies Everywhere by Phyllis Root
Love You Hoo by Rachel Bright
Busy Birdies (A Busy Book) by John Schindel

Little Bird, Little Bird

By Sue Penix

Little bird, little bird
Fly around.
Up to the sky and
down to the ground.

Little bird, little bird
Flap your wings
Open your beak
And sweetly sing.

Little bird, little bird
Fly to your nest
Now it is time
To take a rest.

GLORIOUS GRASS

Grass holds many sensory treasures for even the youngest child to enjoy. Little ones enjoy a fresh air snooze while lying on a carpet of grass. Crawlers find special delight in exploring the feel of grass on their knees and hands as they rove about the play yard. Toddlers experience the texture of grass when they pull and pinch its blades and when it tickles their feet. There are many ways you can help young children experience the glories of grass—here are just a few:

- Take off shoes and walk barefoot.
- Place babies directly on the grass for tummy time.
- Take nap time outside in a grassy area.
- Place grass clippings in clay or fingerpaint.
- Fill a low container with lukewarm water and add grass for water play.
- Poke grass blades in the holes of a colander.
- Find several small unbreakable containers and fill a few with grass. Encourage children to pour or transfer grass from one container to the other.

DID YOU KNOW? For some young children, engaging in grass play or other experiences with natural materials may be difficult because of tactile sensitivities.

Researcher Becky Delvecchio offers practical tips for supporting children who have tactile sensitivities:

1. Introduce materials with one texture at a time rather than mixing them together,
2. Provide natural materials regularly and for extended periods of time, and
3. Offer mittens or gloves for children to wear while playing with the natural objects.

Delvecchio also recommends that in addition to spending large chunks of time out in nature, sensitive children can enjoy nature play by reading books about nature together and sharing what you notice in nature from a window or the door.[5]

---

5. DelVecchio, B. & Ferguson, S. "Nature Play with Sensitive Children." *Teaching Young Children.* 13(4), 6, 2020.

Grass Stew

Toddlers are just getting into pretend play. Invite little ones to cook up some pretend grass stew: Place a pot and small pitcher of water along with a big wooden spoon on the grass. Encourage toddlers to pour the water into the pot and add bits and pieces of grass, dandelions, leaves, or other found natural treasures, and then give the 'stew' mixture a big stir.

PATTERNS OF PLAY

- TURNING & STOPPING: Children's stirring actions are physical. While they observe the mixture swirling in the bowl they are creating with the play pattern of *Turning & Stopping*.

Grass Bracelet

Encourage the use of multiple nature materials by having children create nature bracelets. This activity is easy to do and all you need is duct tape and the outdoors. To create the nature bracelet, position a piece of duct tape sticky-side-out loosely around children's wrists, ankles, and even waists. Go outside and let the children search for just the right bits and pieces of nature to collect and then press onto the duct tape. Suggest rolling on the grass or rubbing their hands over a tree trunk to see what the duct tape will collect. Once back inside, cut the duct tape off the children's bodies, glue onto a piece of wood or cardboard, and display in an area visible to the children.

Bamboo Marking

Bamboo is a perfect natural material for young children's explorations because of its unique texture and shape. (The stems are hollow when cut into pieces.) Although bamboo is native to Mexico and Central America, the plant can be found in many parts of the United States and Canada. Bamboo can also be purchased in art, garden, or decor stores.

Encourage little ones to experiment with making marks on the bamboo using mediums such as Tempera paint, crayons, or markers. Or, offer children a few natural sponges along with Tempera paint and small pieces of bamboo. Don't instruct children on what to do—just sit back and let the experimentation begin!

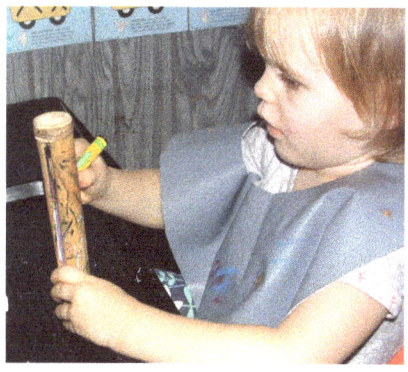

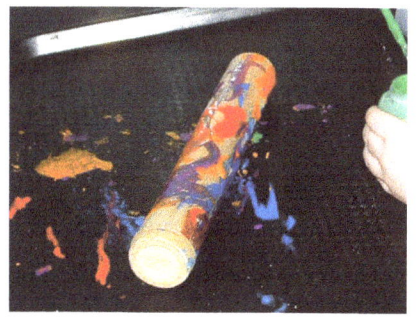

The glory of gardening: hands in the dirt, head in the sun, heart with nature.
–Alfred Austin

GROWING GARDENS

There are many opportunities to connect children to gardens. The easiest way is to follow their lead. Observe their interests and listen to their voices. The garden is more than planting and harvesting. As teachers, we have a tendency to put "learning" at the top of the list when thinking about a garden's primary purpose. Although children will learn about all sorts of things (i.e., what plants need to grow), focus on the joy rather than on aligning academic standards to gardening experiences. Gardens offer continuous joy with the discovery of the first seedling popping from the ground, the thrill of picking a handful of strawberries warmed by the sun, or biting into a sour kumquat peel, only to be surprised by its sweet interior. Gardening can also extend to many other aspects of play. For example, place a painting easel and Tempera paint near the pumpkin patch or invite children to paint directly on the fat pumpkins growing on a vine. Or, in a quiet corner of the garden, place a braided rug, a couple of pillows, and a basket of storybooks.

Be in the mindset that young children are very exuberant so plants may accidently be pulled up by their roots!

Use these times as teachable moments, take a breath, and help children replant the disrupted and displaced plant as you model tender care. To keep your garden blossoming and plentiful throughout the growing season, try planting more than is needed so when children invariably pull up the plants, you will still have enough at harvest time.

PATTERNS OF PLAY

- **HIDING & REVEALING:** Children bury and dig up seeds, roots and some vegetables.
- **CARRYING & PLACING:** Provide containers for carrying and placing in the garden to promote this Pattern of Play.

Mini-Gardens

Planting a garden with toddlers can be as simple as a small shallow container in the classroom, or some pots outside, next to the classroom door. Place the mini-gardens where children can easily access them.

Portable Gardens

A portable garden means you can carry or roll the garden to any location you want and at any time you desire due to the weather, climate, sun exposure, or other situations (i.e., moving it from the big playground to the infant's play area). Examples of portable gardens are pots on wheels or a child's wagon. A small box (2' by 2' square with a 3" edge) can be built. Add coasters and you have a perfect portable garden!

Note: For a perfect growing soil, mix 1/3 peat moss, 1/3 vermiculite, and 1/3 blended compost. These ingredients can be purchased at any garden center or home improvement store and may be available at the local grocery store.

TIPS FOR GARDENING SUCCESS WITH VERY YOUNG CHILDREN

- Arrange pots or low-to-the-ground planter boxes so children can directly interact with the vegetable plants and flowers. Leave the stroller behind.

- Include ready-to-eat herbs in the garden for children to pluck and enjoy throughout the growing season. Be sure to plant fast-growing herbs (i.e., basil, parsley, mint) and in large quantities. There's no such thing as too much basil or parsley for quick harvesting and snacking.

- Plant aromatic herbs in various parts of the garden. Separate the aromatic herbs (i.e., mint, rosemary, basil, chives) into the four corners of the garden. Doing so will allow children to experience their beautiful smells individually.

- All plants in a child's garden should be completely edible. If unsure about plant safety, check with a local garden center or the Internet for a list of poisonous and non-poisonous plants.

- Remember, the garden plot does not have to be all in one spot. Consider splitting up the garden and perhaps having a tomato garden all in one spot or plant lettuce in a huge pot. By splitting up the garden into "specialty" gardens, you have more control over where the garden will be located (i.e., sunny spot or in a semi-shade area).

- If your program has limited space, consider a container or dish garden. Container gardens are portable and can be easily transported between your indoor and outdoor environments. Consider placing outdoor container gardens next to the mud kitchen, dramatic play area, sand box or by a sensory table where children can easily pick and use the plant material during their play.

- Include a digging spot in the garden.

Sensory Gardens

For full sensory gardens that stimulate all of the senses choose aromatic flowers for the sense of smell, edible herbs and plants for the sense of taste, textured plants such as lamb's ear for the sense of feel, native grasses that rustle in the breeze for the auditory sense and colorful wildflowers for the sense of sight. You might include a pathway that also provides some sensory engagement for the children to meander and explore.

HINT
Mint is prolific and grows very fast.

Install mint along your pathway or as a section of the pathway and invite children to tramp about in the mint patch, releasing a beautiful fragrance. Mint is resilient so don't worry, it will quickly revive and continue to flourish.

EDIBLE FLOWERS FOR YOUNG CHILDREN'S GARDENS	
Calendula	Dandelions
Lavender	Violets/Violas
Sage Flowers	Nasturtiums
Zucchini Blossoms	Rosemary

TYPES OF GARDENS		
HERB (Oregano, Basil, Lemongrass)	**VEGETABLE** (Tomato, Pumpkin, Cucumber)	**FAIRY** (Fairies, Stone Houses, Bridges)
POLLINATOR/FLOWER (Nectar & Pollen)	**SENSORY** (Lavender, Mint)	**COMBINATION** (Both Flowers & Vegetables)
STORYBOOK (Story Characters on Posts)	**SUCCULENT** (Spiral Aloe, Jade Plant)	**BUTTERFLY** (Habitat for Each Life Stage)
DISH GARDENS (Small Containers)	**ROCK GARDENS** (Rock Sculptures)	**WALL** (Hanging Garden Built on Wall)

Wall Gardens

If your program has limited outdoor ground space, consider a wall garden. These little gardens are containers that have been attached to a wall or perhaps a fence. They are ideal for planting two or three small plants or herbs. Tin cans or plastic liter bottles are the perfect size for the containers.

Note: Small containers require daily watering as they have a tendency to dry out quickly, especially during hot summer months.

Pallet Herb Gardens

A reclaimed pallet makes an excellent herb garden because it has ready-made sections for different types of herbs. Place pallets in the garden, or on a flat surface you have designated. After filling each section with potting soil, plant either herb seeds or starter plants. It's as simple as that! For a little pizzazz, invite children to paint the pallet with Tempera using oversized paintbrushes. Once dry (and the children are gone for the day), add a coat of clear varnish to seal.

Note: When using reclaimed pallets for children's gardens, check for a stamp indicating if the pallet has been chemically pretreated. Be sure to select a clean pallet with no chips, cracks or splinters. If needed, sand the pallet before using it with children.

Kitchen Scrap Gardens

These unique kinds of gardens do not require much. Just save kitchen scraps that you would normally throw in the garbage or put in the compost, plus containers, dirt, and water. Here are a few ideas:

Celery
Trim a bunch of celery 3" or so above its base. Place in a shallow dish of water. Leaves should grow out of the center in a week and tiny roots will sprout from the bottom. Peel away any rotting stalks as the plant grows. Be sure to change water every other day to reduce the chance of rotting stalks.

Beets
Slice top ½" from fresh beet with the greens still attached. Trim the greens leaving approximately ¼" of stem. Rinse the beet top, and then place in a shallow dish of water. Little shoots should appear within several days.

Basil
Trim several stalks from a basil plant, pinching off the larger leaves from the stalks' top. Submerge the cut ends in water. The bottoms will darken, and after about 2 weeks, small roots should emerge.

Garlic
Tightly pack several cloves in a small container and cover them with water. Roots should appear within the first few days, and then sprouts will emerge from the cloves' tops within a week.

In addition to the fun learning experience of quickly growing plants, kitchen scrap gardens reinforce the sustainable living concepts of recycling and reusing. Follow these additional tips for successful kitchen scrap gardening:

- Use organic produce as it seems to work better than conventionally grown variety.

- Place the kitchen scrap garden in a warm spot where it will get as much sun as possible.

- Check the water level every day and change water every third day to eliminate odor.

- Transfer rooted plants to containers with potted soil for further growth.

Use a spray bottle to moisten the plant leaves every few days.

STUPENDOUS STICKS

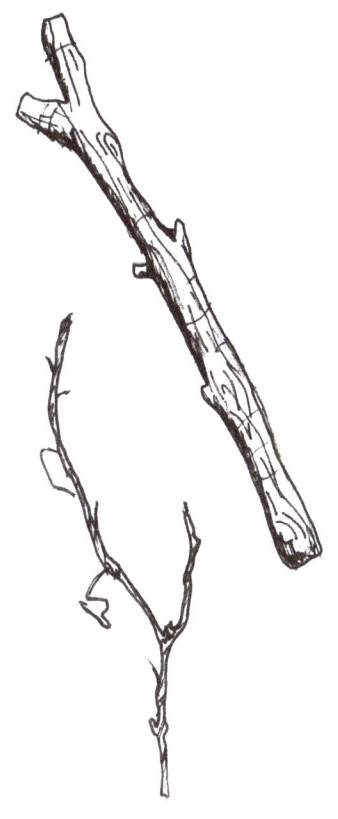

Inducted into the National Toy Hall of Fame in 2008, the stick has forever been cultivating young children's imaginations and creativity. To an adult, a stick may seem insignificant, or even mundane. To a child, however, a stick can become anything. It offers wide-ranging possibilities for creative and pretend play, as it becomes a storyline prop such as a magical fairy wand, fishing pole to catch a big whale, construction tool to make a skyscraper, or pounding drumstick in a marching parade. Consider adding sticks to the indoor and outdoor environments to encourage older toddlers' imaginative play and creativity.

Offer a variety of sticks such as hardwoods, softwoods, driftwoods, and bamboo in different lengths and widths. Include interesting pieces of wood with knots, twists, and bends. The children's search for the perfect stick to use in their creation is part of the fun. When combined, attached, or glued with other materials, the stick becomes a creative representation of children's imaginations. Here are a few materials and ideas to use with sticks to encourage creativity in stick play.

STICK PLAY WEAVING MATERIALS			
Ribbon	String	Yarn	Corks
Paint	Raffia	Pinecones	Paper (all kinds)
Leaves	Clay	Mud	Colored Tape
Seed Pods	Beads	Lace	Other Sticks
Fabric Scraps	Silk Flowers	Real Flowers	Large Buttons

Stick Weavings

Find a few Y-shaped sticks. (They are easier to find than one would think—just be on the lookout!) The Y-shaped sticks should be small enough for little hands to manage. For safety, blunt cut any sharp or pointed ends from the sticks. In a small basket, put several types of weaving materials such as small bits of ribbons, short pieces of yarn, and thin strips of cloth that have been cut to approximately 3" in length. Encourage children to arrange the materials on the stick in any fashion they choose: weave, string, place, or wrap. How they do it isn't important. What is important is the process of attaching the materials to the stick.

PATTERNS OF PLAY

- **ATTACHING & DETACHING:** Children put together and take apart combinations of materials, using the stick as the base.

There are many natural materials that can be woven with sticks such as twine, willow branches, ornamental grasses, long and narrow leaves, and ivy.

Collage on a Stick

Find a stick with many branches. Place a variety of lightweight natural materials (i.e., grass clippings, moss, and raffia) in a basket and provide squeezable glue. Watch as children enjoy messing about. Once dry, attach a piece of string to the collage and hang it in the classroom.

Painted Sticks

Instead of painting on paper, try painting sticks. Young children love to experiment with paint and delight in finding new and alternative surfaces on which to apply paint (including themselves). Paint sticks with a brush, sponge, or even fingers. Another interesting way to paint sticks is to place paint in a container and dip the ends of the stick into the paint. As toddlers lift the stick out of the paint, they are captivated by the way the paint rolls down the stick or plops on the tabletop.

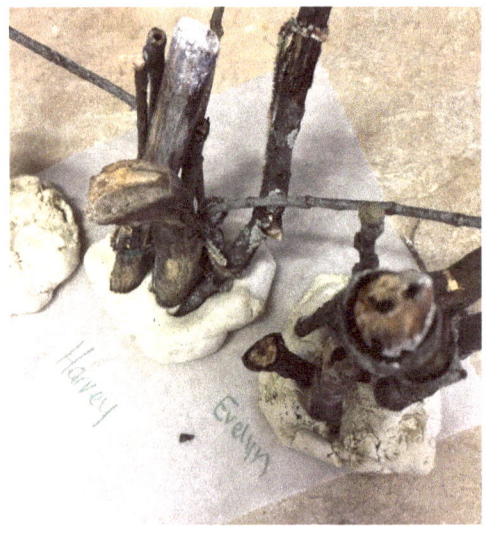

Sticky Stick Sculptures

Provide a variety of colored and sticky tapes for toddlers to wrap around a stick. Since there is no right or wrong way to wrap the stick, it is an ideal art medium for the very young child. Hang the beautifully wrapped stick creations from the classroom ceiling or display in a window. Or, encourage children to make sticky stick sculptures. All you need are small pieces of sticks and natural clay. The children do the rest!

SAFETY WITH STICKS

You may be uneasy with letting young children explore sticks. As with the introduction of any new item, weigh the benefits against the risks. Research has shown that playing with natural objects such as sticks or other natural materials has many benefits over traditional toys. Traditional toys are typically one-use (i.e., the ball is rolling on the floor), and sticks are open-ended and multifunctional. A stick can be rolled, tapped, stacked, and lined up on the floor. Stick play also offers sensory experiences that traditional plastic toys do not. Here are some ideas to get you started:

- Limit the number of sticks available. Start with one, to begin.

- Find plain and tiny sticks without little branches coming out from their sides. Use sticks that do not have pointy ends. If you are unable to find blunt-ended sticks, cut off the sharp ends with a knife and then use heavy-duty sandpaper to sand the ends so they are smooth.

- When introducing stick play, begin with a very small group of children so they can be closely supervised. Begin by sitting while playing with tiny sticks. Model for the children how to handle a stick and be safe with it.

Develop simple rules, which will need to be continuously repeated, such as:
- Walk while holding a stick.
- Hold only 1 stick at a time.
- Sticks are for hands, not for mouths.

Before including sticks in the classroom, it's important to consider the group of children with whom you are currently working. To introduce sticks as a material in the classroom, you might want to begin by reading *Not a Stick* by Antoinette Portis. This is a story about a pig that is imaginatively using a stick for all sorts of props. The narrator tells the pig to be "careful with the stick" and "not point the stick," but the pig keeps insisting it is not a stick. With a slightly older child, this storybook can open up many conversations about safely playing with sticks.

PRETTY PINECONES

Pinecones are a great natural material to use with young children. Easy to find and absolutely free, the many different species of pinecones vary dramatically in appearance and size, and are visually and tactically diverse.

> Pinecones: They're little treasures that drop from the trees and wait like new friends to be found. Pinecones show us that we are all different, all beautiful, and all perfect in our imperfection.
>
> —Christy Wheat

Pinecone Palooza

Long and short ones, fat and skinny ones, pinecones come in a variety of shapes and sizes. Place an assortment of pinecones in a basket along with a variety of containers. Children will enjoy sorting the pinecones and placing them in the containers.

Pretty Pinecone Presents

Bits and pieces of yarn or rattan, ribbons, and laces wrapped on pinecones make intriguing works of art. Place a basket of pinecones alongside a basket filled with wrapping materials and watch the beautiful creations begin. Give the lovely child-created pinecones back to the pine tree with a gifting ceremony by placing the wrapped Pinecones in the tree's boughs or at its base.

PATTERNS OF PLAY

- ATTACHING & DETACHING: When creating Pretty Pinecone Presents, children wrap a variety of items around the pinecone then remove items, exhibiting the *Attaching & Detaching* play pattern.

Shake and Make Pinecones

Fill three large-sized bowls or containers with three different colors of Tempera paint. Select a variety of different-sized pinecones. Invite children to drop the pinecones into the container of paint and gently shake the container back and forth.

As an alternative to bowls, use a plastic kiddie pool. Position a piece of white paper that fits the bottom of the pool. Invite several children to drop their pinecones onto the paper and then gently shake the pool by grabbing its side and moving back and forth. Here are a few hints for a successful and joyful experience:

- If using a smaller container such as a box lid, it is best to have only one child at a time shake the container.

- Add a few squirts of liquid soap to the paint for quick and easy cleanup.

- Use primary colors (i.e., red, yellow, blue) for interesting color transformations as the primary colors blend into secondary colors (i.e., orange, green, purple).

PATTERNS OF PLAY

- **MAKING & UNMAKING:** Children make new paint colors as they repeatedly shake the box lid back and forth.

- **PROPELLING & HINDERING:** When children shake the box, they are propelling pinecones within the lid that stops the trajectory or movement of the object.

Kerplink—Kerplunk

Young children love to drop things . . . over and over again. As early childhood educators, we often observe this recognizable and repeatable behavior action. A child dropping food off the side of the highchair tray may be an exhibit of the Play Pattern called *Propelling & Hindering*, which is the primary urge of picking things up and moving them. Tossing broccoli from the highchair may also be the child's essential urge to change her visual perspective of the broccoli simply through the movement of it.

Dropping food on the floor could be considered wasteful. And after picking up the food for the umpteenth time, it could be perceived as an annoying incident for some teachers. So, here's an idea. Once mealtime is over, why not offer opportunities to practice this new trajectory game created with the broccoli? Place a few containers such as a metal pot, plastic bucket, or cardboard box on the floor near the high chair. Give the child two or three large-sized pinecones and encourage dropping them overboard into the containers.

Will children throw the pinecones? Yes they will! They are practicing the Play Pattern of trajectory or *Propelling & Hindering*. Will flying pinecones hurt anyone? Probably not, since children's arm strength prevents them from throwing at any great distance and with any amount of velocity.

The children will most likely want to drop the pinecones into the supplied containers over and over again and listen to the different sounds as they land. This experience gives wee ones the opportunity to practice with the law of gravity as well as cause and effect.

Turkey Baster Pinecones

Wee ones are fascinated with squeezing the paint from the container and watching it splash on the pinecone.

Here's how to set up the experience:

1. Place a container of non-toxic paint, pinecones, and a turkey baster on a tray.

2. Demonstrate to the child how to squeeze the paint up into the baster and propel out onto the pinecone.

The dandelion does not stop growing, because it is told it is a weed.

The dandelion does not care what others see.

It says, 'One day, they'll be making wishes upon me.'

—B. Atkinson

DELIGHTFUL DANDELIONS

Whether you appreciate the wish-making lore of a dandelion that releases its seeds to float through the air, or dread the inevitable weed that seems to invade everything from cracks in the sidewalk to vast fields, there's no denying the charming fascination that young children have with these plants.

Dandelion Soup

Toddlers love pretending to cook. Dandelions are plentiful in the early spring and make wonderful natural materials for children to add to their pretend stews and soups. Simply provide a variety of bowls, spoons, pots and pans and a little water. Soon your little chefs will be creating a delightful dandelion soup.

Dandelion Dough

Make a batch of dandelion dough using the following easy-to-make recipe:

1 Cup flour
½ Cup salt
1 Tablespoon cream of tartar
1 Cup water
1 ½ Tablespoons vegetable oil
5 to 12 Dandelion flowers with petals removed from dandelion heads

Instructions
1. Place all ingredients into a large pot and place on a medium heat.

2. Stir constantly until dough forms a ball and does not stick to the sides of the pot.

3. Place dough on a plate and flatten it out to cool. Be careful, it is very hot.

4. Once cooled, place in an airtight container and store in the refrigerator.

Dandelion Weaving

Place a basket of dandelions with long stems next to a colander. Your toddlers will soon discover they can stick the stems of the dandelion into the holes of an overturned colander.

PATTERNS OF PLAY

- **ATTACHING & DETACHING:** Children repeat the actions of placing dandelion stems into the colander holes and then removing them.

Dandelion Bouquets

Take young children to an open field during early spring and soon you'll observe them finding all the dandelions that have come into bloom. Young children are naturally curious about these yellow delights and pick them to make beautiful bouquets. Toddlers dance around waving dandelions in the air as if to say, "Welcome spring I've been waiting for you!" Provide the children with small baskets or paper bags with handles to collect dandelions to bring back to the classroom to explore further.

Line 'Em Up

Since dandelions are very plentiful in the spring, pick a pile of them, bring them back to the classroom, and encourage little ones to line the dandelions up in a row, move them and line them up again. When children engage in this activity, they are practicing the pattern of play of *Carrying & Placing* since they are positioning the dandelions in an orderly way.

Dandelion Fluff (Tune: I'm a Little Teapot)

Author Unknown

I'm a little dandelion tiny and small
(crouch down low)

Growing in the sunshine, stretching big and tall! *(slowly stand up)*

My bright yellow flowers turns to fluff, *(make circle with arms above head)*

Waiting for you to come and puff! *(hands over mouth and blow)*

I'm a little dandelion tiny and small
(crouch down low)

Growing in the sunshine, stretching big and tall! *(slowly stand up)*

All my little seeds will float away, *(dance fingers in the air)*

Floating on the wind, this bright sunny day!

PLAYFUL PUMPKINS

Pumpkins are one of autumn's delights. They come in a variety of colors, shapes, and sizes offering abundant possibilities for the classroom and outdoor play. Some varieties of pumpkins (and gourds) even have bumps and ridges, which are perfect for kinesthetic as well as physical exploration. They are perfect to place on the floor for even the youngest child to explore. Pumpkins can be stacked, rolled, and small ones can be carried from place to place.

Pumpkin Boats

Place miniature pumpkins in a shallow bin of water or in the water table, then stand back and observe how children discover floating pumpkins.

Pumpkin Painting

Pumpkins and paint are a wonderful combination that children can experience both inside and outside. One way to paint with pumpkins is to spread out newspaper in a long row on the ground. Invite children to dip small pumpkins into paint and then roll the pumpkins across the newspaper. Be prepared for children to be covered in paint, as this is a fun but messy experience!

Carrying and Stacking Pumpkins

Young children like the notion of being strong and doing "hard" work, especially when it involves transporting or stacking objects. Simply provide easy-to-handle pumpkins and watch the action begin and continue as children repeat carrying and stacking actions over and over again. For easier stacking, select pumpkins having flat spots. Cutting off the stems also facilitates children's ease of stacking.

PATTERNS OF PLAY

- **CARRYING & PLACING:** Children repeat the actions of picking up, transporting and stacking pumpkins.

- **TURNING & STOPPING:** Children roll, twist, and spin the pumpkins either on the ground or in a container of water.

- **PROPELLING & HINDERING:** Children roll pumpkins covered in paint across newspaper.

Books About Pumpkins

It's Pumpkin Day, Mouse! by Laura Numeroff
In the Middle of Fall by Kevin Henkes
Five Little Pumpkins Came Back by Dan Yaccarino

Pumpkin Patch Song
By Sue Penix

Hi-ho Hi-ho

To the pumpkin patch we go.

We'll pick a pumpkin big and fat.

Paint it's face and give it a hat.

Hi-ho Hi-ho

To the pumpkin patch we go.

SUNNY SUNFLOWERS

Sunflowers are classic crowd pleasers—especially for the very young! Sunflowers are able to reach great heights in a single growing season and now come in a variety of sizes and colors. Grow short sunflowers such as Teddy Bear Dwarf and Sunspot, which rarely grow over 2 feet tall, or try your green thumb at growing tall sunflowers such as Mammoth Grey Stripe, which can reach 15 feet. Pick your bloom colors: traditional shades of yellow plus shades of orange, red, and even white. You can even leave sunflowers standing after the growing season to attract pretty goldfinches or other birds who will come and enjoy a winter snack.

Light Table Sunflower

Find a sunflower and cut the head from the stem as close as you can. Use double stick tape to adhere the sunflower head to the light table. Provide a variety of interesting materials that are the same color as the sunflower and encourage children to design and create using the sunflower as inspiration.

Sunflower Prints

Cut several sunflower heads while visiting the sunflower patch. Place the sunflower heads on the floor, in the grass, or in a sensory bin and let the children explore. They will naturally begin plucking the petals from the sunflower heads. Once there are a bunch of loose petals, place the petals on a piece of white paper. Provide wooden crab mallets and encourage lots of pounding. The pounding causes the petals to disintegrate and the flower's color bleeds onto the white paper. Lift off remaining flower pieces and voila! You may also use thin white fabric, in place of paper.

Pulling Petals

Young children are naturally drawn to pulling the petals from flowers, looking at them, and dropping them on the ground, table, or floor. Sunflowers with their large heads make the perfect petal-pulling flower.

PATTERNS OF PLAY

- **ATTACHING & DETACHING:** Children detach flower petals that are attached to the sunflower heads.

- **MAKING & UNMAKING:** When children add the pulled petals to mud pie or soup, they are making and unmaking.

Books About Sunflowers

Sunflower House by Eve Bunting

This Is the Sunflower by Lola M. Schaefer

Little Sunflower by Igloo Books

Beautiful Sunflowers Full-Color Picture Book by Fabulous Book Press

WIGGLY WORMS

Wiggly and squiggly worms seem to appear out of nowhere after a good rain! Young children are mesmerized by these little creatures and absolutely love investigating their mysterious appearance. If worms are not to be found in the local neighborhood, then they may have to be purchased. If you buy worms, Red Wigglers are the best because they are very active and can be obtained at fishing supply or local gardening stores.

Worm Watching

Exuberant young children love to get up close to watch worms wiggle. On occasion, hands and feet may inadvertently squish a worm. Support children's natural curiosity by getting down low alongside them and talking to them about what they see. Show children how to be gentle so as not to hurt the worm. Extend this exploration by providing magnifying glasses for more close-up investigations. Once the children are finished observing, gently place the worms back in the grass or dirt.

Worm Digging

Digging in the dirt can lead to the wonderful world of worms in their natural habitat. To encourage worm digging, set aside a special place in the outdoor classroom for digging. Place a bin with shovels and maybe even a bug box or two for the children to observe worms up close before returning them to the digging hole.

PATTERNS OF PLAY

- HIDING & REVEALING: Children find and uncover worms in the dirt then return the worms to their original location.

Worm Terrarium

Bring worms into the classroom for a few days to observe. They can be kept in a covered terrarium with moist dirt, a few leaves, and some sticks. Spray the terrarium's surface with a little water if it appears to be drying out. Earthworms or Red Wigglers are the best type of worm for little hands to hold.

Note: Bloodworms, which are sometimes used by anglers, can sting, so avoid bringing this variety into the classroom.

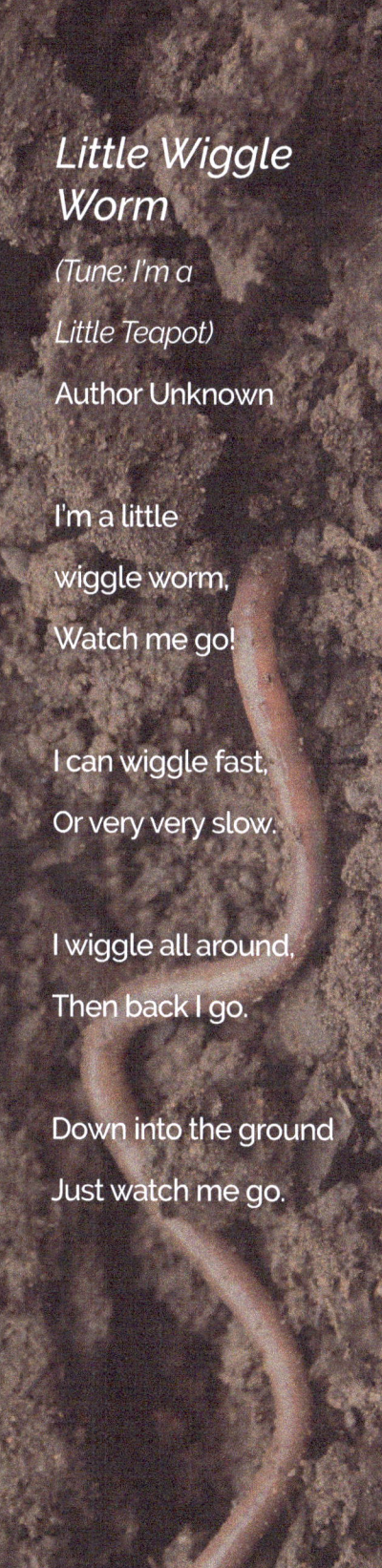

Little Wiggle Worm

(Tune: *I'm a Little Teapot*)

Author Unknown

I'm a little wiggle worm,
Watch me go!

I can wiggle fast,
Or very very slow.

I wiggle all around,
Then back I go.

Down into the ground
Just watch me go.

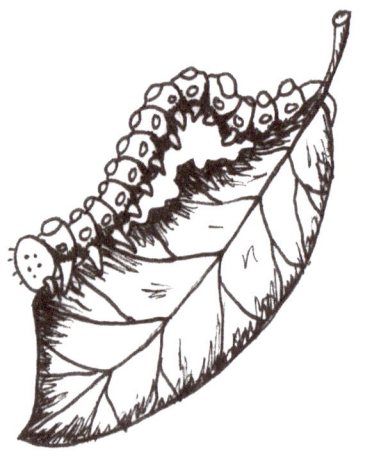

FLUTTERBY BUTTERFLIES

Young children are captivated by butterflies. Encourage these beautiful floating creatures to visit your outdoor space by planting perennial plants that butterflies use for shelter and food. Visit your local nursery or garden shop for native plant seedlings. There are certain plants that are good for the larval (caterpillar) stage of growth and others that are better for the adult (butterfly) stage.

PLANTS FOR CATERPILLARS VS. BUTTERFLIES	
Caterpillar (Larval Stage)	**Butterfly** (Adult Stage)
• Milkweed* • Lupine • Fennel • Currants • Gooseberries • Veronica	• Columbine • Lavender • Marigold • Oregano • Rosemary • Shasta Daisy

*Some species of milkweed can be toxic to humans, especially if eaten in large amounts, so it is best to plant out of the reach of little hands. You may want to consider placing a low fence around your butterfly garden so little ones can observe safely.

Additional plants that are good for butterfly gardens include sunflowers, parsley, chives, and dill. Here are some tips to attract butterflies:

- Butterflies need trees and shrubs to shelter them from wind. Offer a hiding place, and a spot to land or roost.

- Butterflies need a nearby source of water including mud puddles, which provide salt and nutrients from the earth and contribute to their health.

- Sunlight is an important ingredient for attracting butterflies. Because butterflies cannot fly when their bodies are cold, it is important to position pollinator plants in full sunlight.

> *Butterflies like to roost on rocks warmed by the sun so try positioning a few rocks in the garden or near a concrete or paved sidewalk that gets at least six hours of warm sun each day.*

The Fuzzy Caterpillar

(Tune: "The Eeensy Weensy Spider")

Author Unknown

The fuzzy caterpillar
Curled upon a leaf,

Spun her little chrysalis
And then fell asleep.

While she was sleeping, she dreamed that she could fly,

And later when she woke up
She was a butterfly!

Caterpillar Crawl

Have your little ones pretend to be hungry caterpillars hunting for food. Find a nice grassy spot and let your toddlers and twos crawl through the blades of grass in search of delicious leaves.

Books About Caterpillars

The Very Hungry Caterpillar by Eric Carle

The Little Caterpillar by Bill Martin Jr.

Caterpillar to Butterfly by The American Museum of Natural History, Melissa Stewart

Butterfly Dance

Place a bin of silk scarves by the garden for children to pretend they are butterflies flying in the wind.

PATTERNS OF PLAY

- **TURNING & STOPPING:** Children twirl and spin as they dance like butterflies.

Butterfly Feeders

Help feed and support your local butterflies by placing slices of overripe fruit (such as bananas, oranges, and papaya) on a shallow tray or dish. Frisbees make wonderful hanging butterfly feeders. Simply flip the frisbee upside down, punch holes along the rim, and add colorful yarn or string for hanging. Sponges soaked in a simple sugar syrup give butterflies an energy boost and can be used as an alternative to fruits.

Butterfly Simple Syrup Recipe
4 Cups water
1 Cup white cane sugar

Put sugar and water into a medium-sized saucepan and bring to a boil, stirring to dissolve the sugar completely. Cool thoroughly before using.

Note: Do not use honey or raw sugar for this recipe as they are harmful to both butterflies and hummingbirds.

CONNECTING WITH
CONCOCTIONS

Our lives are interconnected with nature. We delight in its sounds, sights, smells, tastes, and textures. Nature's gifts of infinite forms, colors, and patterns offer children and adults abundant opportunities for exploration, observation, play, and hands-on experience. As teachers of infants, toddlers, and two-year-olds, we can help children actively engage and create through concoctions—an easy and rewarding way for children to play with nature.

GETTING STARTED WITH CONCOCTING

Create a place, inside or out, dedicated to concocting. For young ones, it's best to begin on a very small scale and introduce just a few materials and tools at one time. Gradually add new materials to the concocting station. Try adding larger items to the station such as heavy-duty cardboard tubes, plastic gutters, PVC pipes, or cove molding, to support imaginative thinking. As always, be sure the materials offered are developmentally appropriate and safe, and that play is well supervised.

Hint: Add interesting ingredients for children's concoctions such as cinnamon sticks or coriander seeds. Buying cinnamon sticks online and in bulk significantly reduces the cost. Also, you may find that purchasing cinnamon sticks (and cinnamon-scented pinecones) during the holiday season saves money.

How does one plan for curiosity, initiative, persistence, risk-taking, and resilience? Learning (in nature) often occurs without being taught and without the direct intervention of an adult.

—Wendy Banning and Ginny Sullivan

If the concocting station is outside, there are few worries about the mess. Indoor concoction stations can present a challenge. Here are a few suggestions to minimize mess:

- Think small and contain the play to just one surface with a couple of tools and containers. Provide a maximum of two types of mixing components (i.e., water and liquid soap; sand and clay).

- Place the concocting station in an out-of-the way place (i.e., in a corner or the back of the room) in a low-traffic area.

- Protect the floor and table surface by covering them. A plastic picnic tablecloth with felt-type backing works well.

- Have small dustpans, brooms, and wastebaskets on hand for easy cleanup.

- Provide smocks, aprons, or cover-ups for children to protect their clothing.

Vary the surfaces for concocting. Try these ideas: terra-cotta tile, tree stumps, large rocks, tree bark and bamboo mats.

NATURAL MATERIALS FOR CONCOCTING			
Grass Clippings	Dirt/Sand	Large Pinecones	Corn Husks
Clay	Water	Small Twigs	Tree Bark
Driftwood	Leaves	Ice Cubes	Seeds
Large Seashells	Dandelions	Flower Petals	Snow
Corn Husks	Tree Bark	Large Tree Pods	Mud

Mortar and Pestle: Concocting Tool

The mortar and pestle is a simple (yet versatile) tool for concocting with wee hands. Use a mortar and pestle to smash, grind, mix, and pound, all wonderful behavior actions that young children absolutely love to do. A mortar is a container shaped like a bowl. A pestle is a stick-type device used for grinding the substance contained in the mortar.

Hint: Place a small tray with low sides under the mortar and pestle to catch objects that escape the bowl!

PATTERNS OF PLAY

- **MAKING & UNMAKING:** Children repeat pounding, grinding and stirring actions that change the state of the material placed in the mortar.

MATERIALS FOR PULVERIZING

Dried Corn Kernels	Sterilized Egg Shells	Garlic Bulbs	Pinecones
Ochre (Soft Stone)	Onion Skins	Lavender	Basil
Anise Seeds	Grass Clippings	Carrot Tops	Cumin Seeds

CHALK CONCOCTIONS

Purchase chalk from a reputable company. This ensures the chalk is made from quality ingredients and lead free. Also, be sure the chalk meets the highest ratings on safety testing. Before purchasing, check for any recalls on the chalk. You may also want to choose a dust-less chalk, which minimizes dust in the air that may be an irritant to children with allergies or pre-existing breathing conditions.

Chalk Ice

It's cool to the touch and leaves multi-colored masterpieces on the sidewalk.

1 Cup Cornstarch
1 Cup Water
4 Drops Food Coloring, Washable Paints, or Liquid Watercolors

1. Mix cornstarch and water together to form a smooth mixture.

2. Pour into ice cube trays, muffin tins, or egg cartons that have been washed.

3. Add drops of food coloring, washable paints, or liquid watercolors into each individual mold. Stir carefully.

4. Place a wooden Popsicle stick in the mixture and place in the freezer until frozen.

Be sure children only hold chalk ice by the wooden Popsicle stick, to avoid children's hands getting too cold.

Chalk Clay

Add texture and a little variety to clay. Offer different-colored sticks of chalk along with a mortar and pestle and encourage children to crush up the sticks into small pieces. After the chalk is crushed up, invite little ones to press and mix the ground chalk into the clay.

Chalk Sand

Mix pulverized chalk with sand. Using slightly wet cotton balls, swabs, or tissues, dip into the mixture of chalk sand and then swipe onto a surface such as paper, cardboard, or sandpaper. Or, just let the children decide how they want to manipulate and use the chalk sand. Prepare for a mess, but a beautiful mess!

CONNECTING WITH CONCOCTIONS   227

Wet Chalk

A wet chalk concoction can be made simply by dipping sidewalk chalk into water and letting it sit for 2 minutes. After the chalk is wet, try encouraging children to apply the chalk to dark-colored construction paper or a piece of cardboard. Another idea is for children to explore making marks with the wet chalk on different textures of sandpaper.

A variation of this concoction is to soak chalk overnight in a solution of a third of a cup of sugar mixed with one cup of water.

The sugar water intensifies the color of the chalk.

PATTERNS OF PLAY

- **MAKING & UNMAKING:** When children transform the dry chalk to wet chalk by dipping it in water, they engage in the Pattern of Play called *Making & Unmaking*.

PAINT CONCOCTIONS

One example of concocting and building connections to the natural world is through the age-old art of making paint from plants and berries. When certain berries are in season, encourage children to taste a variety, such as blueberries, strawberries, huckleberries, and blackberries. After the tasting party, use a few of the berries to make healthy popsicles or smoothies.

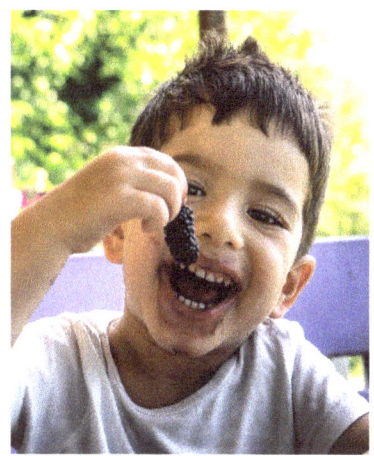  

Berry Paint

Use a mortar and pestle to pulverize the fruit. Then add a small amount of water or distilled vinegar. The berry paint may not be as bright or have the same vitality as Tempera paint, but it has a beauty and subtlety all its own. Experimenting with berry paint is exciting for the two-year-old, as the blueberry paint may appear pink when it is wet but will turn a blue color when dry. Plop small amounts of salt granules on top of the wet berry paint to see what happens. Berry paint also takes on different looks depending on the material to which it is applied. Offer small squares of different types of paper for children to explore the differences in the paint's look. Other materials to use with berry painting include muslin or cotton cloth. If you are averse to using food for making paint, use the hulls of the strawberries, which are inedible and usually discarded or composted.

Note: Many berries will stain clothing and tabletops, so be sure children wear protective clothing and cover tables with newspapers, old sheets, or tablecloths.

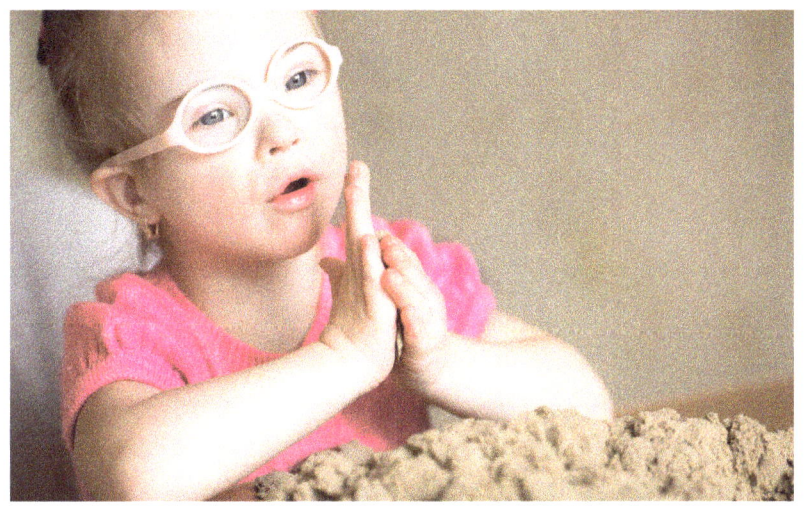

SAND CONCOCTIONS

Concocting with sand and paint is an exciting experience for toddlers. What happens when you squeeze a little bit of blue and a small amount of yellow together in sand? Toddlers will be transfixed as they watch a new color appear before their very eyes. Put a small amount of white play sand in a low flat container and place it on a plastic tablecloth (or some other type of covering) on the floor or table. Fill several squeezable bottles with brightly colored water that, when combined, make a recognizable color.

Blue + Yellow = Green
Blue + Red = Purple
Yellow + Red = Orange

Invite children to squeeze the different-colored water combinations onto the sand and mix it with their hands. They will soon discover that blue and yellow make green or blue and red make purple. With little ones, it is not important that they memorize the color name.

NOTE
This isn't a lesson in color naming or recognizing the different colors. What is important is the excitement of making a new color . . . it's like magic!

Older toddlers may enjoy hearing the story of *Little Blue and Little Yellow* by Leo Lionni.

TEXTURE CONCOCTIONS

Natural materials such as herbs, flower petals, twigs, grass, straw, dirt, sand, clay, and leaves can all become ingredients in creating concoctions, potions, stews, and brews. Invite little ones to gather an array of natural materials from outside and provide mixing ingredients (i.e., water or paint). Add recycled materials such as sawdust, dried coffee grounds, flower petals, orange peels, or leaves to clay, sand, or water to create textured concoctions with new colors and smells.

CONNECTING WITH CONCOCTIONS   233

Fairy Stew

A little water, flower petals, leaves, and a sprinkling of fairy dust (sand) and imagination are all that is needed to create fairy stew. Mix well, pour into small containers, and set the snack out under a tree or bush for fairies, elves, or gnomes to enjoy.

Real Potions

Spring and summer bring an explosion of colors as flowers come into bloom. Colorful flower petals are ideal in children's magic potions. Offer children flower heads (flowers with the stems cut off) and encourage them to rip and tear the petals into small pieces. Since no potion is complete without some type of liquid, stir and swirl the petal pieces into a small pot or bowl of water.

Meadow Paint

Sprinkle and mix grass clippings into different colors of Tempera paint and add a few drops of liquid glue as well. Cover a table with large pieces of cardboard and place a few containers of the meadow paint for the children to create three-dimensional and scented paintings.

Potpourri Dough

With its many shapes, colors, smells, and textures, potpourri is a unique and inexpensive material. Add potpourri to homemade playdough for a fun-smelling art experience.

MORE IS LESS
When offering concoction materials for little ones, begin by limiting your offerings to 1 or 2 different types of materials.

Increase the variety once the children have exhausted their explorations.

Herbal Play Dough

To make dough:

1½ Cups Flour
½ Cup Salt
½ Cup Water
Assorted Non-Toxic Fresh Herbs (Rosemary, Mint, Basil, Thyme, Parsley)

1. Mix together flour and salt.
2. Add water.
3. Knead the dough ingredients together and, if necessary, add a little more water.
4. Invite children to tear fresh herbs into small pieces.
5. Knead in fresh herbs.

This dough holds up and keeps for several weeks in an airtight container.

PART 3

PUTTING IT ALL
TOGETHER

> The education of even a very small child does not aim at preparing him for school, but for life.
>
> –Maria Montessori

PUTTING IT ALL TOGETHER: ENVIRONMENT, MATERIALS, AND PEDAGOGY

As these activities demonstrate, nature supports teachers in facilitating meaningful child-led experiences, which lead to children's learning, and acquiring understandings.

It is only when children take the lead in their own play discoveries that true understanding takes place. A simple but effective way to facilitate this process is to observe and document what you observe.

With The Honeycomb Hypothesis in mind, observations should be focused on the following questions:

1. What are the observable repetitive actions (or Patterns of Play) that children are exhibiting?

2. How can I promote these actions (i.e., offering natural materials; reshaping or rearranging environments, having meaning-full conversations)?

You will support children's Patterns of Play by implementing the pedagogical practices of (1) pure exploration; (2) narrated exploration; and, (3) transformational exploration discussed earlier in this book (see pages 34-35).

The Honey Bee's Learning Environment

The honey bee's favorite place to buzz about is in a wildflower garden. The honey bee is happiest with lots and lots of flowers—the more, the better.

Is the same true for the young honey bees in your classroom? Is _more_ better? In some respects, the answer to this question is a resounding "yes" but in other ways, the answer is absolutely "no." Let's take a look at when more is better.

BEAUTY IS BETTER. Like all of us, children need beauty, and benefit from it in their lives. Here are some simple tips for infusing more beauty into the classroom:

1. Create more beautiful classrooms by reducing the amount of plastic in the environment. Although plastic is easily sanitized, it holds little aesthetic value. It is typically smooth to the touch and has minimal visual interest.

   In the case of plastic, more is not better.

2. Increase beauty in the classroom by reducing the amount of primary colors in the classroom. Research has found that children's exposure to too many primary colors can have a negative impact on both learning and behavior. Substitute more natural and neutral colors such as beige, cream, and ivory. Remember neutral colors when choosing furniture, rugs and carpets, draperies, and even the classroom containers.

   In the case of primary colors, more is not better.

3. Improve the beauty of classroom walls by remembering that less is more. Consider yourself a curator in an art gallery—a person who is intentional about what should be displayed, where artwork should be hung, and how it is framed. Honor children's work by displaying it with grace and beauty.

   In the case of classroom wall displays, more is not better.

ACTIVE IS BETTER. Just like honey bees, young children are very active and love flying about the classroom, eagerly exploring every nook and cranny available to them.

As the Honey Gardener cares for and tends to the garden and hive, so does the teacher prepare and tend to the classroom environment by cultivating special places where young honey bees' interests and developmental needs are met through play. With careful attention, design your classroom so that the space supports children's movement needs.

When allowing for freedom of movement, more is better.

SIMPLICITY IS BETTER. There's a growing trend in society to simplify. Yet, this message of simplicity has not made its way to young children's classrooms.

Children's brains are wired to make connections. If the environment is too chaotic, it is difficult (if not impossible) for children to make connections. Young children are incapable of deciphering all the stuff in an over-laden classroom. When they are unable to filter out the overwhelming stimuli, young honey bees are challenged to construct mental models (or honeycombs) because they are unable to accommodate or assimilate all the data points they are receiving. Simplicity is essential. Here are a few tips to keep it simple in your classroom.

- Minimize wall displays and be intentional about what is put on the walls. Be sure there is a reason for the display and that it coordinates with the adjoining classroom space. The majority of displays should be child-made.

- Limit the amount of stuff and the number of containers placed on shelves. For the very young child, it's best to not overcrowd the shelving space. Rather, put out a few selected materials and rotate them often.

- Select rugs with little or no pattern that are neutral in color. These types of rugs create a palette that makes it easier for children to focus while playing on the floor.

- Reduce the amount of stuff hanging from the ceiling, and have a reason for what you do hang up. One good reason for hanging objects from the ceiling is to designate a space. For example, a piece of drapery cloth or an empty lamp shade hung over the table in the house area draws children's attention to that space.

- Consider the infant's viewpoint. In the infant room, teachers often hang a mobile over the changing area so children can see it while diapers are being changed. Be sure the mobile offers a good viewpoint for the infant. Improve infant's views by adding three-dimensional objects.

In the case of stuff in the classroom, more is not better.

The Honeycomb Hypothesis and Piaget: Exploring to Learn

Much of The Honeycomb Hypothesis is founded on the work of Swiss psychologist Jean Piaget. (1896-1980) He believed children are scientists who eagerly and actively interact with the environment and its materials. Through hands-on activities and experiences like the ones we have shared in this book, young children construct mental models of their world. Piaget believed that, as children grow and learn, their mental models are continually organized and reorganized to incorporate new understandings and associations. This occurs naturally and abundantly when children are at play, free to explore the world around them. Piaget described children's process of discovery and meaning-making through the concepts of assimilation and accommodation.

ASSIMILATION	ACCOMMODATION
• Process of acquiring new information and incorporating it into an existing schema. • Reshapes environmental input to fit existing schema.	• Process of altering ideas based on newly gathered information and incorporating it into a pre-existing schema OR building a new schema. • Modifies or adds schema(s) to readjust for environmental input.[6]

These processes of assimilation and accommodation result in what Piaget called "intellectual adaptation"—the formation of new understandings. As children acquire new experiences and observations, they accommodate the new information by adapting. This happens continually as children explore, try, adjust, and explore again. As Piaget put it, "Adaptation is an equilibrium between assimilation and accommodation." This experiential knowledge cannot be given or taught to children, but it is obtained and incorporated through their own unique exploration and process.

6. Piaget, J. & Inhelder, B. *The Psychology of the Child.* New York, NY: Basic Books, 1969.

The Honey Bee's Flight Pattern to Understanding

The flight of honey bees foraging for pollen is instinctive and focused. Although it may look chaotic, the flight of the honey bee is actually deliberate and intentional, with one goal: to bring pollen back to the honeycomb. The honey bee's innate radar always points home, to the hive. These busy "flying about" actions of the honey bee are much like young children's purposeful and repetitive movements when they are engaged in Patterns of Play. While it may not be obvious, children's "flight patterns"—like the honey bee's—are intentional and purposeful. Young children have the innate urge to explore. Through their play, they gather information about the world around them. Children are compelled to seek understandings, and to assimilate and accommodate the experiences and observations they gather. In their play, they naturally fill up and grow what is collected in their "honeycomb" brains. Children's urges to explore are insatiable. Because acquiring understandings is personally unique to each child, there can be no global blueprint or for children's learning.

As an early childhood educator, your role is not to provide a blueprint for a one-size-fits-all environment. Your role is to create environments (both inside and outside) where young honey bees are offered abundant places and opportunities to gather bits and pieces of information—especially with natural materials of all kinds, shapes, and sizes—for authentic play experiences. Your role is not to pull or push children into learning, but to let them lead the way. Your job is to follow along in their footsteps, to listen, observe, and support the discoveries inherent in child-led play.

Novelty is the Pedagogy of the Third Teacher

It is widely held in early childhood education that the environment is the "third teacher." The environment supports children's learning when educators create engaging, novel learning spaces (both inside and out), through the experiences and materials they offer.

Research has shown that our brains are wired to be more highly engaged with novel objects or experiences, and that novelty-seeking is a fundamental behavior found in most organisms with a nervous system.[7]

When children play with something they have never experienced before, they experience what Piaget referred to as "disequilibrium"—they are uncomfortable, unsure, uncertain, or out-of-balance. Their instinctive response is to try to find equilibrium in their mental models, through the processes of accommodating or assimilating the new material. Piaget asserted that children's motivation to learn is driven by their need to find balance in their mental models.

If we accept that novelty-seeking is an inherent characteristic of children, and if we accept that restoring equilibrium is a motivator of learning, we begin to understand how to best support children's learning, both through our pedagogical practices and our offerings of novelty through experiences, materials and environments.

SUPPORTING YOUNG HONEY BEES IN FINDING BALANCE. Some children approach novel items with great eagerness and enthusiasm. We call this Exuberant Curiosity. Other children will hesitate before playing with a new object or engaging in a new experience. We call this Quiet Unsureness.

If we observe closely and quietly, there is an interesting moment when a child experiences disequilibrium, and is motivated instinctively to restore equilibrium. For example, when Jeremiah encounters a snake for the first time, he may be immediately curious about the shiny skin and quickly reach out to touch it. Jeremiah has Exuberant Curiosity. Latoya, on the other hand, sees the snake and immediately withdraws with obvious hesitation. She has Quiet Unsureness.

As educators, our immediate response to Latoya's uncertainty might be to force her into Exuberant Curiosity by saying "Go ahead, don't be scared, it will not hurt you." But, if we remember that Latoya is finding balance in her mental models by adjusting, adapting, or building new cells in her honeycomb brain, we respect her process. She needs time and space, free from adult interference, in order to find her own equilibrium in her own unique way. It is very important to honor a child's inclination—whether Exuberant Curiosity or

7. Ostroff, W. "The Cognitive Science and Neuroscience of Young Children's Curiosity." *Exchange*, May/June, 22-26, 2020.

Quiet Unsureness—as a key component in their learning. Respecting the child's natural response and inclination allows them to experience something new on their own terms, and be supported at the same time.

DISEQUILIBRIUM MOTIVATES LEARNING. So, how do we support children in disequilibrium? How can we honor the moment of either Quiet Unsureness or Exuberant Curiosity? How do we embrace the notion that disequilibrium is the motivator for learning? There are two vital gifts we can give to young children to support this growth: novelty and autonomy.

Gift of Novelty
There is a circular set of three events that occur with the process of learning: (1) Novel objects and experiences evoke curiosity. (2) Curiosity promotes interest. (3) Interest facilitates learning. These three events are interconnected, dependent upon each other, and happen simultaneously. The igniter to this learning process is novelty.

By its very essence, nature is novel. Providing experiences and materials from nature helps to ensure novelty and increases children's insatiable urge to move, explore and create. Novelty encourages the Patterns of Play, helping children incorporate new understandings and find equilibrium.

Gift of Autonomy
Giving young children autonomy means that, as early childhood professionals, we give them the right to take charge of their own learning. Autonomy is the notion that children are capable of their self-direction and, consequently, perfectly able to develop their own approach to learning. Piaget calls this spontaneous learning and it occurs when the child learns by himself and of his own accord. Spontaneous learning can only happen when adults get out of the way.

Novelty and autonomy go hand in hand. When we honor the way in which a child encounters and engages with the environment, we are giving the gift of autonomy. Offering these gifts to our youngest of children gives them wings to fly, worlds to explore, and honeycombs to build.

AN INVITATION: TAKE FLIGHT WITH HONEY BEES

We offer this book as an alternative to the pedagogy of teaching that originated in the Industrial age and still persists today—an outdated, traditional approach that treats the child as an empty vessel to be filled by the teacher's knowledge. We feel these teaching methods undermine children's natural creativity and stunt their potential.

Open your brain and let me (as the adult) fill it with what I think you should learn. Your interests, little one, are not my interests. Your ideas cannot possibly be as important as my ideas. Your knowledge must be contained to achieving standards, to knowing (but not understanding) the letters of the alphabet, numbers and numerals, colors and shapes, and all things considered worthy of being "academic."

This stifling pedagogy diminishes children's capacity to thrive as passionate, natural learners. Children grow up knowing the *answers* to questions, but not understanding *how* to question. They grow up knowing how to color within the lines, but not realizing it is within their power to break or transform these lines. Children grow up knowing what to think but not how to think.

The good news is that children are resilient and wise, and if given the opportunity, can construct their own understandings and build their own creativity through the brilliance of play—especially with Earth's natural elements. When we trust the innate wisdom of young children and let them lead the way with Patterns of Play, early childhood educators lay the foundation for innovative thinking and brilliant minds.

By truly listening to children's hearts and understanding their innate desires to play, we honor them. Through this honor and respect, we are saying that infants, toddlers, and two-year-old children are more than little beings who need to be coddled. We are saying that their inborn urges matter; we are encouraging their curiosity and need to explore their world. Because we acknowledge children as capable of guiding their own play, we follow where they lead, without imposing our rules of engagement or our ideas of what should be known.

It is time to give back the birthright of every little honey bee—the power of flight through the power of play. It is our hope that this book has inspired you to open your heart, let in the child's heart, and inspire little honey bees to be their best, fly their highest, and journey wherever their dreams take them.

WHEREVER MY DREAMS TAKE ME

Sasha's dad had been reading her stories about dreams.

In the middle of the night, Sasha went to her parents' bed and got in between them.

When they got up in the morning, the mother saw that Sasha had on her swimming suit, pajamas, jeans, and parka.

Mom said, "Why do you have all those clothes on?"

Sasha replied, "Because I just want to be ready to go wherever my dreams take me."

– A Story from Docia Zavikovsky

ACKNOWLEDGMENTS

We are deeply grateful to the many people who graciously shared their amazing ideas, expert knowledge, and valued opinions for this book. Your dedication and devotion to young children, their right to play in natural spaces, and your commitment to this inalienable right is truly inspirational. We wholeheartedly thank you and wish only the best for continued happiness and success in working with the youngest of children.

- Daniela Arbizzi
- Megan Asche
- Jamie Atencio
- Meredith L. Baker
- Jody Barger
- Amy Beam
- Stephanie Bennett
- Laura Bilbrey
- Moon Bishop
- Melissa Brown
- Christine Burkholder
- Jenni Caldwell
- Tom Chairomonte
- Paula Christine
- Martha Cosgrove
- Sandy Crosser
- Stacey David
- Cecilia Dunn
- Sue Evans
- Rixa Evershed
- Amanda Eversley
- Vicky Flessner
- Monica French
- Svane Frode
- Courtney Gardner
- Erica Gajewski
- Michelle Gajewski
- Erin Goodloe
- Tori Griggs
- Lyndsey Hellyn
- Sabrina Hetland
- Nicole Hill
- Melissa Hughes
- Joyce Jones
- Celeste Joyner
- Kate Kincaid

Jennifer Kinkel
Christy Knight
Andrea Knudsen
Nick Langbehn
Sandy Langbehn
Michael Leeman
Lisa Lewis
Cheri Lindsley
Tammy Lockwood
Kelly Lucchesi
Karen Madigan
Molly McClanahan
Lauren McGee
Roseann Murphy
Corye Nelson
Clare Nugent
Danielle Olsen
Patricia Green Pappas
Jenny Parker
Karin Pavelek
Tiffany Pearsall
Hilary Roberts King
Lesley Romanoff

Katie Rooney
Rosa Parks Early Childhood Center
Susan Sandstrom
Beth Savitz
Pam Schiller
Sonia Semana
Kelsey Shackelford
Susan Shepardson
Christopher Sickels
Margo Sipes
Donna Smith
Hayley Smith
Zlata Stankovic-Ramirez
Elisa Switzer
The Curiosity Approach
Debra Ward
Linda Watts
Monica Wiedel-Lubinski

ABOUT THE AUTHORS

Sandra Duncan

Sue Penix

Sally Haughey

ABOUT THE AUTHORS

SANDRA DUNCAN works to assure the miracle and magic of childhood through indoor and outdoor classroom environments that are intentionally designed to connect young children to their classrooms, communities, and neighborhoods. Dr. Duncan is an international consultant, author of six books focused on the environmental design of early childhood classrooms, designer of two furniture collections called Sense of Place and Sense of Place for Wee Ones, and adjunct faculty at Nova Southeastern University. Sandra has designed university courses on indoor and outdoor learning environments, collaborating with architects, interior designers and educators to create extraordinary places and possibilities for children and students of all ages. Sandra is a water-bug, which means she thoroughly enjoys being on or near the water—especially saltwater. Sandra's idea of a terrific time is to walk along the seashore, find gifts from the sea, and share these beautiful treasures with her granddaughter, Sierra.

SUE PENIX has served in the field of Early Childhood Education for over 40 years and holds a degree in Early Childhood Education with a minor in Special Education. She currently works for the Baltimore City Child Care Resource Center as an Infant and Toddler Specialist, trainer and a Nature Educator Consultant. Sue is a facilitator of a total nature emergence training program for childcare programs throughout Baltimore City, and serves as the Board President for the Eastern Region Association of Forest and Nature Schools. Sue has presented numerous sessions on Nature Based Learning at local and national conferences and is a certified trainer for the Growing Up Wild Curriculum through the Department of Natural Resources in Maryland. Her backyard is a certified natural wildlife habitat through the National Wildlife Federation. Sue is also an avid camper and the very proud grandmother of two little girls, Adalena and Julie who love and adore nature.

SALLY HAUGHEY is the CEO and Founder of Fairy Dust Teaching. Fairy Dust Teaching is built on the passion for the wonder and magic of early childhood the idea that young children have the right to play, to be collaborators in learning, and to dream. After 20 years of successfully teaching in various school settings, she has committed herself on what she loves most: Empowering and Inspiring Educators! Her focus is to provide a deeper level of service and training that help educators own their true teaching self. Sally has now worked with over 100,000 educators in her online e-courses and workshops. Sally loves to watercolor paint and spend time creating beautiful messes with her grandsons.

RESOURCES

Atherton, F. & Nutbrown, C. "Schematic Pedagogy: Supporting One Child's Learning at Home and in a Group." *International Journal of Early Years Education.* 24(1), 63-79 (2016).

Bedard, T. "Levels, Spaces, and Holes at the Sensory Table." *Exchange.* January/February (2016).

Beloglovsky, M. & Daly, L. *Early Learning Theories Made Visible.* St. Paul, MN: Redleaf Press, 2015.

Brown, S. & Vaughan, C. *Play: How it Shapes the Brain, Opens the Imagination, and Invigorates the Soul.* New York: Avery, 2009.

Carson, R. & Pratt, C. *The Sense of Wonder: A Celebration of Nature for Parents and Children.* New York: Harper & Row, 1965.

Chawla, L. "Benefits of Nature Contact for Children." *Journal of Planning Literature.* 30(4), 433-452. (2015).

Christakis, Erika. *The Importance of Being Little.* New York: Penguin Random House, 2016.

Crawford, Maggie. "The Importance of Natural Toys and the Environment for Children." Retrieved from www.bhoomilearningcommunity.org

Cuppens, V., Rosenow, N., & Wike, J. *Learning with Nature Idea Book: Creating Nurturing Outdoor Spaces for Children.* Lincoln, NE: Arbor Day Foundation, 2009.

Curtis, D. & Jaboneta, N. *Children's Lively Minds. Schema Theory Made Visible.* St. Paul, MN: Redleaf Press, 2019.

DeViney, J., Duncan, S., Harris, S., Rosenberry, L., Rody, M., & Rosenberry, L. *Inspiring Spaces for Young Children.* Silver Springs, MD: Gryphon House, 2010.

Duncan, S. & Bilezikian, G. "Heart-Centered Environmental Design: A Fresh Perspective." *Exchange.* November/December, 2019.

Duncan, S., Martin, J., & Kreth, R. *Rethinking the Classroom Landscape: Creating Environments that Connect Young Children, Families, and Communities.* Lewisville, NC: Gryphon House, 2016.

Duncan, S., Martin, J., & Haughey, S. *Through a Child's Eyes: How Classroom Design Inspires Learning and Wonder.* Lewisville, NC: Gryphon House, 2018.

Duncan, S. & Martin, J. *Bringing the Outside In: Ideas for Creating Nature-Based Experiences for Young Children.* Lincoln, NE: Exchange Press, 2019.

Edwards, C., Gandini, L., & Forman, G. (Eds.). *The Hundred Languages of Children: The Reggio Emilia Experience in Transforming Education,* 3rd Ed. Santa Barbara, CA: Prager/ABC-CLIO, 2012.

Finlay, B. Brett & Arrieta, Marie-Claire. *Let Them Eat Dirt: Saving Your Child from an Oversanitized World.* Chapel Hill, NC: Algonquin Books, 2016.

Fjortoft, I. "The Natural Environment as a Playground for Children: The Impact of Outdoor Play Activities in Pre-primary School Children." *Early Childhood Education Journal.* 29(2): 111-117. (2001).

Fruin, Hannah. "Muddy Play: Reflections on Young Children's Outdoor Learning in an Urban Setting." *Young Children.* (75)1: 68-75. (2020).

Goldschmied, Elinor. *People Under Three: Young People in Day Care.* Philadelphia, PA: Routledge, 2004.

Greenman, J. *Caring Spaces, Learning Places: Children's Environments That Work.* Lincoln, NE: Exchange Press, 2019.

Halford, G. *Children's Understanding: The Development of Mental Models.* New York, NY: Psychology Press, 1993.

Hanscom, A. *Balanced and Barefoot: How Unrestricted Outdoor Play Makes for Strong, Confident, and Capable Children.* Oakland, CA: New Harbinger Publications, 2016.

Haughey, S. "The Twelve Senses." Retrieved from www.fairydustteaching.com

Jana, L. *The Toddler Brain: Nurture the Skills Today That Will Shape Your Child's Tomorrow.* Boston, MA: Da Capo Press, 2017.

Johnson, J. & Joiner, J., Eds. *Going Out Is Going In.* Ventura, CA: Patagonia, 2015.

Kellert, S. & Calabrese, E. "The Practice of Biophilic Design." Retrieved from www.biophilic-design.com

Kellert, S. & Wilson, E. *The Biophilia Hypothesis.* Washington, D.C.: Island Press, 1995.

Kellert, S. *Children and Nature: Psychological, Sociocultural, and Evolutionary Investigations.* Cambridge, MA: MIT Press, 2002.

Keeler, Rusty. *Seasons of Play: Natural Environments of Wonder.* Beltsville, MD: Gryphon House, 2016.

Kiewra, C., & Veselack, E. "Playing with Nature: Supporting Preschoolers' Creativity in Natural Outdoor Classrooms." *The International Journal of Early Childhood Environmental Education,* 4(1), 70-95. (2016).

Kimmerer, Robin. *Braiding Sweetgrass: Indigenous Wisdom, Scientific Knowledge, and the Teachings of Plants.* Minneapolis, MN: Milkweed Editions, 2015.

Lewin-Benham, A. *Twelve Best Practices for Early Childhood Education: Integrating Reggio and Other Inspired Approaches.* New York: Teachers College Press, 2011.

Lindon, J. & Brodie, K. *Understanding Child Development 0-8 Years: Linking Theory and Practice,* 4th Ed. London: Hoder Education, 2016.

Louv, R. *Last Child in the Woods: Saving our Children from Nature-Deficit Disorder.* Chapel Hill, NC: Algonquin Books, 2008.

McLeod, S. *Jean Piaget's Theory of Cognitive Development.* Retrieved from www.simplypsychology.org

Mooney, C. *Theories of Childhood: An Introduction to Dewey, Montessori, Erikson, Piaget, & Vygotsky,* 2nd Ed. St. Paul, MN: Redleaf Press, 2013.

Nabhan, G. & Trimble, S. *The Geography of Childhood: Why Children Need Wild Places.* Boston, MA: Beacon Press, 1994.

Nelson, E. *Cultivating Outdoor Classrooms: Designing and Implementing Child-Centered Learning Environments.* St. Paul, MN: Redleaf Press, 2012.

Nutbrown, C. *Threads of Thinking, Young Children Learning and the Role of Early Education.* Newbury Park, CA: Sage Publications, 2006.

Ohanesian, Diane. *Snuggle Down Deep.* New York, NY: Little Bee Books, 2018.

Pelo, Ann. *The Goodness of Rain: Developing an Ecological Identity in Young Children.* Lincoln, NE: Exchange Press, 2018.

Piaget, J. *Play, Dreams, and Imitation in Childhood.* London: Heinemann, 1962.

Piaget, J. *The Origins of Intelligence in Children.* Translated by Margaret Cook. New York: Routledge, 1952.

Piaget, J. *The Construction of Reality in the Child.* New York: Basic Books, 1957.

Piaget, J. & Wolff, P. "Some Aspects of Operations" in *Play and Development: A Symposium.* Edited by Maria Piers. New York: WW Norton, 1972.

Piaget, J. *The Child and Reality: Problems of Genetic Psychology.* New York: Grossman Publishing, 1973.

Rahmani, Parisa & Moheb Naeimeh. "The Effectiveness of Clay Therapy and Narrative Therapy on Anxiety of Preschool Children: A Comparative Study." *Procedia Social and Behavioral Sciences.* 5, 25-27. (2010).

Reid, K. "Counting on It: Early Numeracy Development and the Preschool Child." Australian Council for Educational Research. (2010).

Rivkin, M. *The Great Outdoors: Restoring Children's Rights to Play Outside.* Washington, DC: National Association for the Education of Young Children, 1990.

Rivkin, M. *The Great Outdoors: Advocating for Natural Spaces for Young Children.* Washington, DC: National Association for the Education of Young Children, 2014.

Rosenow, N. *Learning to Love the Earth and Each Other.* Spotlight on Young Children and Nature. Washington, DC: National Association for the Education of Young Children, 2011.

Rosenow, N. *Heart-Centered Teaching Inspired by Nature.* Lincoln, NE: Exchange Press, 2012.

Schlanger, Z. "Dirt has a microbiome, and it may double as an antidepressant." Retrieved from www.qz.com

Slater, A. "Novelty, Familiarity, and Infant Reasoning." *Infant and Child Development,* 13, 353-355. (2004).

Smith, D. and Goldhaber, J. *Poking, Pinching, & Pretending: Documenting Toddlers' Exploration with Clay.* St. Paul, MN: Redleaf Press, 2004.

Stacey, S. *Inquiry-Based Early Learning Environments: Creating, Supporting and Collaborating.* St. Paul, MN: Redleaf Press, 2018.

Thomas, R. Murray. *Comparing Theories of Child Development.* Belmont, CA: Wadsworth Thomson Learning, 2000.

Vygotsky, Lev S. "Imagination and Creativity in Childhood." *Journal of Russian and East European Psychology,* 42:7–97. (2004).

Wadsworth, B. *Piaget's Theory of Cognitive and Affective Development: Foundations of Constructivism.* New York, NY: Longman, 2004.

Ward, J. *I Love Dirt! 52 Activities to Help You and Your Kids Discover the Wonders of Nature.* New York, NY: Penguin Random House, 2008.

Warden, C. *The Potential of a Puddle: Creating Vision and Values for Outdoor Learning.* 2nd Ed. Auchterarder, Scotland: Mindstretchers, 2012.

Wilson, E.O. *Biophilia.* Cambridge, MA: Harvard University Press, 1984.

Wilson, R. "Beauty in the Lives of Children." *Exchange,* March/April. (2014).

CREDITS

Adobe Stock/ alekleks–p.116; Alex–p.116; Amar–p.203 bottom; ancymonek–p.131 bottom; Andy Dean–p.110 bottom; BigBlueStudio–p.12; Bits and Splits–p.144; bryonyphotography–pp.48, 57, 67; Светлана Фарафонова–p.144; Cuarta Vida–p.185; drod26018–p.176 right; dule964–p.216; ELG Photography–p.65 bottom; evamsi–p.180 bottom; gaukharyerk–p.226 top; hakase420–p.199 bottom; hedge1–p.62; igor tsarev–p.169 left; igorkol_ter–p.155 leaves; jacf5244–p.116; jung eon seo/EyeEm–p.142; Kanthita–p.226 bottom; klagyivik–p.22 bottom; krstrbrt–p.61 footprints; Lori Swadley–p.196 right; mangpor2004–p.116; Mario–p.160 bottom left; Mariusz Blach–p.116; marla_singer–p.48; mdbrockmann82–p.136 bottom; miunicaneurona–p.18; nadezhda1906–p.236; Pawel Horazy–p.144; peter_waters–p.144; Primada–p.48; Stacey Xura–p.48; Sherri Lasko Photog.–p.54; Stuart–p.65 top; sapsan777–p.79; Soho A studio–p.81; Tfk creations–p.48; tiagozr–p.160 right; trongnguyen–p.112 top; troyanphoto–p.229 right; Wayne–p.144; William–p.170 middle.

Beth Savitz Little Birds–pp.58 right, 77 left, 210 bottom.

Cecilia Dunn–pp.71 top, 72 bottom, 103 bottom, 177 middle & bottom.

Celeste Joyner–pp.196 left & middle, 197, 198.

Danielle Olsen–pp.177 top, 201 bottom.

Dimensions Education Programs–pp.56 top, 60 bottom.

Eliza Switzer–p.207 bottom.

Fairy Dust Teaching–pp.58 top left, 75, 104, 107, 129 bottom.

Guidecraft–pp.82 top, 235 bottom.

Heidi Duren–pp.105 middle, 111 bottom left, 122 top right, 162 bottom, 163 bottom.

Irvine Nature Preschool–p.165.

Jody Martin–p.192 top.

Kelsey Shackleford–pp.61, 69 bottom, 78 bottom, 91 top left, 138 top, 147, 223, 229 middle, 234 middle.

Kinderoo Children's Academy–pp.71 bottom, 73 top, 73 middle, 99 top right, 106 top left, 143 top, 156 bottom, 176 left, 202 top.

Lindsay Baker–p.201 top.

Little Sunflowers LLC–pp.53 top, 60 top, 73 bottom, 102 top, 105 bottom, 119, 122 bottom right, 129 middle right, 148 bottom, 153 left, 160 top left, 168, 204 middle, 208, 220 top, 233 right.

Lyndsey Hellyn–p.233 left.

Melinda Marshall–pp.99 bottom right, 112 bottom, 126 bottom.

Mia Villavicencio–pp.220 middle, 232.

Nappy/ Children Nature Network–p.92 top.

Paula Jackson–pp.90 top, 153 middle, 154.

Pixabay/ Credutien–p.122 left.

Sabrina Hetland–pp.120 left, 125, 138 bottom.

Samantha Chelo–p.88 bottom.

Sandra Duncan–pp.191 top, 192 bottom, 199 top.

Shutterstock/ aldegonde–p.151 top; Aleksandr Grechanyuk–p.216; AlexSviridov–p.159; Alina Lebed–p.53 bottom; Amy Myers–p.100; Anastasia Tveretinova–p.161 bottom; Andrew Angelov–p.215 bottom; Angelina Tyshkovets–p.195 top; Ann Rodchua–p.187 bottom; Anna Kucherova–p.141 shells; Arina P Habich–p.143 middle; asife–pp.150, 172; biletskiyevgeniy.com–p.116; Boyarko Nadya–p.84 bottom; Breaking The Walls–p.144; captureandcompose–p.48; caseyjadew–p.133 top; Charles Brutlag–p.170 top; Cholpan–p.114 bottom; Cloudy Design–p.241 top right; Cooper T Photography–p.90 bottom; Cozine–pp.116, 139 right, 216; Cre8Le–p.190 top; CreativeJourney–p.141 top; Damian Pawlos–p.231 bottom; Dasha Petrenko–p.89 left; DerekTeo–p.91 right bottom; Eleonora_os–pp.202 bottom, 231 top; Erol Savci–p.229 left; ESB Professional–p.123; Eva Vargyasi–p.33; evgeniarusinova–p.187 top; Evtushkova Olga–p.55 top; ezphoto–p.184 right; fotorawin–p.72 top; gob_cu–pp.105 top, 204 bottom; Halfpoint–pp.87, 157, 170 bottom; Hoopla Haven–p.66; Hua_khai–p.23; I AM JIFFY–p.108; Ignasi Soler–p.163 top; Igor Batenev–p.116; IgorGolovniov–p.121; Igor Kovalenko–p.144; ingae–pp.96, 224; Inna Reznik–pp.74, 78 top, 92 bottom, 149 top; Iryna Inshyna–p.200; JR-50–p.55 bottom; Jordi Prat Puig–p.68 bottom; Julie Hagan–p.215 top; Julija Sulkovska–p.225 top; Junial Enterprises–p.17; Justyna Troc–p.209 top; Karen Hoskins–p.171; KateSun–p.48; KAY4YK–p.120 right; kesipun–p.89 right; Kirlikedi–p.95 left; Kichigin–p.116; Kolomiyets Viktoriya–p.109; Koki Yamada–p.127; kon–p.182; Krisana Antharith–p.211; LanKS–p.216; LenaVolkova–p.235 top.; leopictures–p.93 right; Luxsury–p.85 top left; Mahony–p.180 top; MaLija–p.28; maramorosz–p.91 bottom left; marcin jucha–p.216; Margoya–p.126 top; Maria Symchych–pp.68 top, 140, 194; maxslu–p.234 bottom; Mcimage–pp.111 top, 146; Mehriban A–p.186; MIA Studio–p.183; Monkey Business Images–p.148 top; myrmica–p.95 top right; NataliaL–p.195 bottom; Natee K Jindakum–p.44; Nattapol_Sritongcom–pp.116, 135; ndstudio1982–p.69 top; Neveshkin Nikolay–p.144; NicoleTaklaPhotography–pp.99 left, 225 bottom; Nik Merkulov–p.48; nikkytok–p.214 left; Nikolai Kazakov–p.228; O.C Ritz–p.184 left; Ole.CNX–p.175; Oliver Mohr–p.209 sunflower; Pakhnyushchy–p.48; Patcharida–p.52; Patricia Marks–p.134; Petr Bonek–p.241 top left; photographyfirm–p.216; Pictures_for_You–p.93 left; piriwat–p.188; pixelheadphoto digitalskillet–p.204 top; PLotulitStocker–p.80; Proshkin Aleksandr–p.216; Purino–pp.203 top, 221; P.V.R.Murty–p.88 top; rebvt–p.216; RimDream–p.91 top right; Rina.Chu–p.241 bottom; Rini Slok–p.144; rodimov–p.169 bottom right; Samuel Borges Photography–pp.101 bottom, 159; schankz–pp.22 top, 144; Sergey Zaykov–p.84 top; Shark9208888–p.85 right; slonme–p.116; Somchai_Stock–p.151 bottom; Soonthorn Wongsaita–p.48; sruilk–p.210 top; Statkar–p.95 bottom right; Stock-Photo–p.111 bottom right; stockphotofan1–p.220 bottom; Studio.G photography–p.132; SUKJAI PHOTO–pp.206, 214 right; Suraphong Surachanchai–p.212; Svittlana–p.248; Tagwaran–p.227; TataSerg–p.59; Tatiana Foxy–p.85 bottom left; Tatitta–p.77 top right; TanyaCPhotography–p.91 right middle; Tanya Yatsenko–p.218; The Childhood–pp.114 top, 152; The_Fairhead–p.130; topseller–p.216; T.Photo–p.161 top; Valentyn Volkov–p.50; VALERYIA LUSHCHYNSKAYA–p.230; ViGor Art–p.139 left; Vitalinka–p.103 top; Volodymyr Burdiak–p.144; Volodymyr TVERDOKHLIB–p.64; VojtechVlk–p.94; VUSPhotography.com–p.162 top; Whistlerpedia–p.136 top; WNstock–p.116;

WOVE LOVE–p.86; Wuttichok Panichiwarapun–p.56 bottom; xpixel–p.58 mud; YamabikaY–p.48; Yana Poles–p.118; Yupgi–p.174 bottom; zlikovec–p.166; Zurijeta–p.113; Zzzenia–pp.102 bottom, 190 bottom.

Sue Penix–pp.36, 77 bottom right, 98, 101 top, 110 top, 133 bottom, 153 right, 164 all, 169 top right, 172 all, 191 bottom.

The Curiosity Approach–pp.240 left & right, 242, 243 left & right, 63, 82 bottom, 97, 106 bottom left, 106 right, 112 middle, 129 top left, 129 top right, 131 top, 143 bottom, 149 bottom, 156 top, 174 top, 178, 207 top, 234 top.

Tori Grigg–p.225 middle.

Unsplash/ Markus Spiske–pp.83, 155 top; Christian Bowen–p.124.

Dedication and author photos provided by the authors.

Illustrations by Kaitlyn Nelsen.

Cover credits: Adobe Stock/ andRiU–top right; candy1812–bottom right; CaptureAndCompose–bottom left; cindygoff–top left; Zachary–bottom middle. Shutterstock/ Natee K Jindakum–top middle.

www.ingramcontent.com/pod-product-compliance
Lightning Source LLC
Chambersburg PA
CBHW041240240426
43668CB00023B/2447